MAGNOLIA KITCHEN DESIGN

MAGNOLIA KITCHEN DESIGN

A journey of sweet inspiration

by BERNADETTE GEE

Photography by Lottie Hedley and Bernadette Gee

ALLEN&UNWIN
SYDNEY・MELBOURNE・AUCKLAND・LONDON

Note: Bets uses New Zealand standard measures, including the 15 ml (3 teaspoon) tablespoon. If you are using a 20 ml (4 teaspoon) tablespoon, you may wish to remove a teaspoon of ingredient for each tablespoon specified.

First published in 2020

Text © Bernadette Gee, 2020
Photography © Lottie Hedley 2020, except where listed below

Photography and sketches on pages 37–38 and 41–97
© Bernadette Gee 2020 (unless otherwise credited)

Allen & Unwin
Level 2, 10 College Hill, Freemans Bay
Auckland 1011, New Zealand
Phone: (64 9) 377 3800
Email: auckland@allenandunwin.com
Web: www.allenandunwin.co.nz

83 Alexander Street
Crows Nest NSW 2065, Australia
Phone: (61 2) 8425 0100

A catalogue record for this book is available from the National Library of New Zealand.

ISBN 978 1 98854 742 8
UK ISBN 978 1 92235 145 6

Design by Megan van Staden
Set in Archer and Gotham

Printed in China by C & C Offset Printing Co., Ltd.

1 3 5 7 9 10 8 6 4 2

MIX
Paper from responsible sources
FSC
www.fsc.org
FSC® C008047

Baking with artistic intent

CONTENTS

SINCE WE LAST SPOKE

I wanted to catch y'all up on what has been going on for me and Magnolia Kitchen since I put finger to keyboard for the last book back in 2018 (released in April 2019).

I recently celebrated the first anniversary of *Magnolia Kitchen: Inspired Baking with Personality*. (You should all know by now that the 'personality' in the subtitle is code for I SWEAR IN THE BOOK.) I honestly hadn't even realised that it had been an entire year since it hit the shelves! Someone on Instagram had tagged me in a picture taken when I launched the book at the General Collective Market, adding the words '1 year bookaversary'. To be honest, it was the furthest thing from my mind—on 1 April New Zealand was in its first week of Covid-19 FULL LOCKDOWN. I was busy stressing about the pandemic, juggling kids at home, trying to figure out how Magnolia Kitchen as a business fitted into all the lockdown rules . . . What a time!!

Realising that my book had been out for a whole *year* made me so happy and so overwhelmed all at once. I mean, still selling a year later?! To celebrate, I decided to do a live lockdown reading on Instagram. I lined it up, then I sat in a comfy chair in the sun and read through the chapter titled 'The journey to becoming Magnolia Kitchen'. It was fun to revisit what I had written, and it also brought up so many emotions—all the emotions I felt when I was writing that chapter—and yes *of course* I cried (haha). I haven't yet been able to read it once without crying! I am apparently not alone, though, as a fair few of you have cried reading it too.

While reading the chapter live to you all I realised how much had changed since I wrote it; I actually felt blown away with what I had achieved in that time. So of course it's a no-brainer to fill you in (and who knows—maybe there will be some inspiration in there for someone).

Let's kick off with September 2018 . . . the news was out that I had a book coming and it was so exciting to be sharing that news with my community. It had been hard keeping the secret for about a year while I was writing—I had literally wanted to scream it from the rooftops. Life returned to semi-normal after the book was sent off to the printers and all we had left to do was plan for the launch the following April, which seemed an interminable time away.

My little James started school in October 2018, which was a huge milestone. Actually, before this book comes out even Edward will have been at school for a couple of months. *WHAT?!!* All you school mums—I know you hear me when I say 9 a.m. to 3 p.m. is not enough time to get any real work done. By the time you walk them into school, then get to work and get a coffee and settle in, it's practically 10.30. Then you're up and out by 2.30 p.m. to get a park so you can walk in and wait by the class and have a chat to the teacher . . . I am still adjusting now, and it's halfway through 2020!

I still remember Magnolia Kitchen Sweet Cafe ramping up for Christmas 2018. Christmas always being our busiest crazy time of year, it passed in a blur. By this stage I'd added more tools to my product line alongside my sharp-as-shit scrapers and had released my Magnolia Kitchen icing spatula set, cake detailing palette knives and denim aprons. The ideas around tools, more retail products and merchandise were endless, and also included online courses—of which I now have 16! I have continued to create and develop products throughout 2019–2020 and hope to have a full range of our baking kits available internationally (along with this book) by the end of the year.

Early in January 2019, the news went viral that my book was available for pre-order online in a few places. The fact that I hadn't even offered pre-sales on my website was a bit of a *faux pas*, but I'd underestimated just how keen you'd all be to instantly pre-order my book from wherever you could. I hustled, and a week later got my own pre-sales going through the Magnolia Kitchen online store.

I can't even begin to explain the whirlwind of those early months of pre-sales. People instantly discovered that there were preview recipes available as part of the advertising. One day in January I was working late; having just popped out to get KFC for dinner and parked back at Magnolia Kitchen, I took a quick peek at Instagram—and found that someone had tagged me on a picture of *MY* Signature Rich Chocolate Cake that they had just baked from the preview available online! Nothing—and I really mean *nothing*—could have prepared me for the overwhelming emotional roller-coaster that hit me as I looked at the very first picture of someone making one of my recipes. I literally burst into tears—not upset, just overwhelmed happy tears. I couldn't believe that I had written a book that people were going crazy pre-ordering and waiting *months* to receive AND that someone had actually used my recipe and made it look as perfect as it should. So many emotions, and so much gratitude for how my community had yet again supported another journey within Magnolia Kitchen. The trust everyone has in my products and recipes is just insane but also hugely heart-warming.

There are so many big moments and firsts I have to share, like when Mel from Allen & Unwin turned up at Magnolia Kitchen unexpectedly on a Saturday . . . As I looked up to see her passing the window I saw what she had in her hand! MY BOOK, MY BEAUTIFUL BOOK, IN HARD COPY IN REAL LIFE. I am not ashamed to say that I squealed and shook and cried! I even hugged!! Nothing beats seeing your hard work, the journey of writing, all bound in a neat hardcover book!

For the next while, I watched my book climb to number 7 on Book Depository's OVERALL bestsellers list!! My book, written by me who has no training in baking, who had never written a book before and has no qualifications to my name, was on one of the biggest international booksellers' bestsellers list. If that doesn't sound cool enough, guess who had the number 1 spot . . . Only *Michelle Obama!* Does life get any better? Turns out, this was just the beginning of the firsts for my little book. By the time the book actually launched on 1 April the publisher had already had to have it reprinted because the first print run had sold out *in pre-orders.*

I am not saying all of this to be narcissistic; I just want to share the feelings of overwhelming joy, pride and disbelief at having my book achieve all of this even before it was officially launched, and to say THANK YOU to all of my community, local and international, who believed in my book enough to buy it before even seeing it! That kind of faith is something I will never ever forget. My success, Magnolia Kitchen's success, and my success as an author is all down to my community. Of course it is hugely down to Allen & Unwin too for the trust they put in me.

The week before launch day finally arrived. We took delivery of 800 books; 600 of them had been pre-sold online and I worked all night to sign them, write messages and package them up into courier bags. The rest were earmarked for the event at the General Collective Market on 30 April. That was another crazy ride—I couldn't see the end of the line where customers were waiting to have their copies signed. Selfies, cock and balls (die-hard MK fans will know what that means) and personal messages for an entire day! I had so much fun meeting everyone that day. I was lucky to have all of my staff there, along with my husband Harley and daughter Charlotte, to be my emotional support 'cause that shit was so overwhelming; half the time I thought I was going to spontaneously combust!

As time went on I started to settle into life as an author. There was still so much hype around the book—it was selling out internationally and even managed to be the number 1 book in New Zealand for a couple of weeks—and I decided it was time for a break. I jetted off to Melbourne

This picture is what bribery looks like. Charlotte has grown up so much since the last book, and I really wanted her captured in this one. This is her 'I am only just tolerating you' face and my 'I am enjoying your only-just-toleration way more than I should' face.

with my girls and we lived it up for four days, then they headed home and I stayed on to do a book signing at Dymocks in Melbourne. Another WTF? moment for me—an international signing?! And a REALLY BUSY signing that people lined up for more than two hours for. How on earth did I get here? It showed me again just how strong my online community is. You guys actually keep me going and remind me daily how far I have come, how much Magnolia Kitchen has grown into an international brand. I will be eternally grateful for this journey and to all of you who have made it possible and played a part.

FROM HIGHS TO LOWS

I want to talk through this because I wish someone had talked about it with me. I wish I had known it was coming so I could have put steps in place to not fall so hard.

The comedown from writing the book came fast, and it came hard. For over 18 months, the book had been my focus. The excitement of being approached to write it, then actually having to plan it and write it, then doing the photo shoot with Lottie, then all the other steps and milestones throughout the whole journey: pre-sales, reprints, the launch, the media events, and then finally the well-earned break. What next? I was left in limbo, creatively and emotionally drained, and wondering who I was now. Was I the person who showed up on Instagram? Was I just a mum, a wife? Was I Magnolia Kitchen? Was I an author? I couldn't breathe and I couldn't feel, and I kept bursting into tears randomly. I felt like I had given away so much of what defined me as a person. My friends and family started to worry about me and gently pressed me to see a doctor. I had started feeling like I wanted to *just leave*—to hop in the car and drive away without telling anyone I was going, or for how long or where. I truly imagined this every single day: just driving away from my life, my family and my business. From everything and everyone I loved and who loved me.

It sounds so scary as I type this, but I think it's important to read it in its harsh truth, to understand it for what it was and to also look back and know that I have come through it.

I made a doctor's appointment. I told him all of this and we discussed mood-stabilising drugs to help me find my happy again. He also referred me to a therapist so I could talk through the whys and hows of my feelings. I am eternally thankful to my friend Katie who warned me about mood-stabilisers—that it would get worse before it got better, and I needed to trust that gradually I would adjust and a happy day would shine through. How right she was! It took two weeks of not getting out of bed, not visiting the cafe, but one day I woke up and I FELT HAPPY!! It was such a shock; I immediately messaged Katie to tell her. The most shocking part was that this feeling of happiness was something I hadn't properly felt in a couple of years. I had been riding the highs and living off stress for so long that I hadn't allowed myself to consider what being happy really was.

Gradually the happy days became more frequent and I started to be more open about what I had been through. I think it is so important to normalise these experiences and talk about them openly. It gives people an understanding of where you are at, it allows them to help you and it allows you to feel good about letting them.

Why did this all happen? I came to the realisation that I had placed a lot of importance on being busy, on having deadlines and projects. When all was done I felt like I was without purpose, and it wasn't a feeling I was used to so it sent me into a tailspin. Of course, part of that realisation made me quickly start planning new projects haha, which right or wrong helped me get back on track, along with the medication. I am still medicated today as I am writing this, and I'm okay with that. I feel good about how far I have come; and having the support of my family, friends, staff and online community has been yet another positive. I have learned to accept support when needed.

That pretty much brings us to 2020. Did I mention I'm writing a second book . . . haha, kind of obvious, right? Oh and the other new project was the relocation of Magnolia Kitchen Sweet Cafe! I never thought when I opened in late 2016 that by early 2017 I would have expanded and leased the shop next door as a prep kitchen. Or that by the end of 2019 I would be viewing a premises down the road that would more than triple our floor space. Regardless of my naivety over the growth of Magnolia Kitchen, the time had come to expand.

The negotiations over the new premises took a couple of months and, as these things usually go, the timeline got pushed out to the last week of January. I sketched up the plans for the new space, which was a complete blank canvas: a huge 308-square-metre space with a concrete floor and exposed ceiling beams for a cool industrial look. Oh my, and the windows—morning sun until 11 a.m. and SO much space for activities.

Harley was shitting a brick over the sheer size of the project. The setting-up of the other spaces seemed so fresh in his mind, and to be fair it had only been three years since the first and two years since the second. Luckily he is on board for the Magnolia Kitchen ride, and once I had shown him that I'd done my due diligence, and planned and budgeted everything within an inch of its life, he felt more comfortable. It also helped that for this fit-out I had insisted on budgeting for a project team,

The Home Skills Company, who might I say were AMAZING. They made the whole process seem less daunting and from start to finish the project took just over 2 weeks!!! When it came to the actual move, I was absolutely shocked; we shut the OG Magnolia Kitchen on Monday and Tuesday and had all hands on deck to shift all the kitchen and cafe furniture from one premises to the other. Then reopened on the Wednesday at the new location.

I now had a self-designed, real-life, larger-than-life, MASSIVE new kitchen (perspective—the same size as our previous two premises *put together*), plus a huge Sweet Cafe with a swanky new coffee machine from Atomic and enough space to seat 28 people comfortably (pre-Covid-19 and social distancing, of course). A huge office space for Serena and me, so huge that we sit approximately 6 metres apart. Eight times the storage and stock shelving, and even a back door with a deck for rubbish bin storage!!! I have made Lottie (epic photographer) come back now that we have moved and photograph everything so that I can show off the epic new space in this book. I am so proud of myself and my team: the work that went into this new location was huge to say the least and it all came together with little to no drama.

We opened the new premises officially at the end of February—just in time for a worldwide pandemic! We only got to properly enjoy three weeks of our new space before the social distancing restrictions were announced, and shortly after that New Zealand was swiftly put into a full country-wide lockdown. I don't want to go into too much detail around this, as it is currently still dominating and destroying life across the world. It still seems surreal, and while New Zealand was able to act fast to flatten the curve and reduce the spread I know that so many in my community internationally are still experiencing scary times. My heart goes out to all those affected, on a personal level, on a business level and on a country level. By the time this book hits the shelves I have the highest of hopes that internationally things will be becoming safer and contained. Stay safe and strong, all of you.

As a business owner with a new shop and hugely inflated overheads, ten staff and their families to support and keep safe, along with keeping my own family safe and provided for, it has been a really crazy stressful time with so much unknown. What has been a constant for me is the knowledge that we are all in this together—everyone is scared, anxious, worried and stressed. Remembering that helps a lot! The pandemic has stretched me to the limits of my capabilities as a brand and a business owner. Thinking on my feet. Re-thinking how we do business, what products work and what don't work. What new products I can develop that bring value and comfort to communities. New Zealand has really come together in supporting local businesses, to boost our economy and keep our country going. So much thanks goes out to our community for their continued support of Magnolia Kitchen through these challenging times. We have so far survived this and will continue to do so thanks to you all! I hope that everyone can experience this feeling of comradeship in their countries and towns across the world. With the support of our communities both locally and online, and with humility, education and change, I truly believe that while life may never look the same again it *will* move forward, we will grow together, and that is something we can count on.

To end this catch-up on a high note, I would like to officially introduce you all to Magnolia Kitchen Boutique. The latest venture under the Magnolia Kitchen brand is the result of some creative thinking during lockdown. I had designed the new Magnolia Kitchen space with a small front area that had huge window frontage and opened into the cafe. It was originally intended to be leased out to a florist, but then lockdown happened and everything fell through. I knew that I still wanted flowers to be part of what we did in that empty space—floristry has always been something I wanted to learn—and we also had this burgeoning list of retail products that we now supply and sell through Magnolia Kitchen. Now I *will* say that I am smart enough to know that re-training myself in floristry would be an over-commitment currently (see? I'm learning to rein myself in!), so I needed to hire someone to run this space for me, someone who was passionate about both flowers and Magnolia Kitchen. Then I had a lightbulb moment: guess what Covid-19 had brought home to New Zealand? My darling moon-child Abby (previously appearing in my first book as one of the Magnolia Kitchen cake fluffers). Abby had left us to travel overseas but had returned with no real plans because of the pandemic. She'd been helping us out at Magnolia Kitchen as a 'ring-in', but when I had my lightbulb moment I immediately messaged her to ask if she would be interested in running the space and learning flowers too.

A massive yes from her, and together we have started the new fit-out journey. The space will be brimming with flowers, both fresh and dried, and customers will be able to peruse shelves stocked with all the Magnolia Kitchen merchandise and retail products. Oh, and my books of course. It has been a whirlwind setting up the new Instagram and website, along with shopping for second-hand props, for shelving and interior design ideas! I am thankful that Abby and I are on the same page—the fit-out is low-cost and won't take long to set up. We are going for a mixture of boho, '70s, Scandinavian, minimalist, sleek . . . just cool stuff that we like.

I can't wait to share this new journey with you all! Until the next catch up, *ciao*.

xx Bets

BETS ON TIPS

I know, I know, you might be familiar with some of these tips (a few of them appeared in my first book), but I wanted to upgrade the list and include some new info that I think will add value to your lives. See also the chapter on Calculations and Scaling.

EQUIPMENT TIPS

- **MICROWAVES**—when a recipe says to use your microwave to heat or melt something, please use your discretion on timings. Everyone's microwave is different, and you will be more familiar with your own microwave than me!
- **SCALES**—always weigh *everything*. I use grams so it's nice and easy, even for liquids—YES, EVEN FOR LIQUIDS, AND YES I DO THIS BECAUSE I AM LAZY. Get yourself some electric scales that have grams, and MAKE SURE THEY WEIGH IN HALF-GRAMS. Live the gram life, love the gram life! Metric is where it's at (unless we are talking about cake sizes, then inches are the exception—see page 238 for my chat on that one).
- **SPOONS**— while we are talking about the gram life, BE AWARE that different countries have different measurements for a tablespoon. (Why is this shit so bloody confusing, right?! Can't we just have a universal metric measurement for everything except cakes, which as we know should always be inches.) TO BE CLEAR, when I say a tablespoon I am referring to the 15 ml tablespoon NOT the over-compensating, recipe-ruining 20 ml tablespoons that have infiltrated our kitchens. Side note: I am passionately against the 20 ml tablespoon, simply for the stress-inducing number of people who contacted me querying the tablespoon of salt in my brioche recipe!!!
- **OVENS**—when my recipes specify a temperature but no setting other than 'bake', this is deliberate. Everyone's oven is different, and chances are if I said 'fan bake' or 'convection' then anyone who didn't have these settings would completely avoid the recipe. Use the setting you are comfortable with on YOUR OVEN as long as it says bake. The temperature does not need to be adjusted based on the setting—the recipes are forgiving.
- **COOKING TIMES**—all cooking times are approximate, so please use them as a GUIDE. I recommend that when the baking time is close to finishing, just keep an eye on whatever you are baking. Look for colour, and ALWAYS poke—use your knitting needle or your skewer and insert it into the cake. It will come out clean when your baking is cooked. If you are new around here, I use a metal knitting needle for testing my baking because my mum did this when I was growing

up. The best hacks are passed down through the generations, and this is actually the best way to test the readiness of your baking. If your baking is taking longer than the specified approximate cooking time, don't stress. All ovens and equipment are different.

- **CANDY THERMOMETER**—ELECTRONIC ALWAYS. It is so important to have a good one. I find that the meat thermometers with the probe on a wire are best; just make sure the temperature range goes high enough for sugar syrup (Italian meringue buttercream needs the syrup heating to 122°C/251°F; don't say I didn't tell you). Also try to get one that has an alarm that you can set to beep when your syrup (or whatever you are thermometering) reaches the desired temp. I use the Hygiplas Multistem Probe (hehe *probe*).

GENERAL BRAIN DUMP OF TIPS

- **LINING CAKE TINS**—grease tins with cooking spray or butter and line them with baking paper. I cut a circle for the base, then a thin strip to go around the inside edge—this means you don't have to wrangle the baking paper up the sides of the tin and risk getting baking paper baked into your cake.
- **SIFTING**—unless I say you *must* do it in the recipe then don't worry about it. Do sift cocoa 'cause it's lumpy, sugar if required, and baking soda always.
- **WEIGHING TINS**—if you're using cake tins that are the same style (shape and weight), divide your mixture between the tins and weigh each one to ensure that your cakes will be even. If you're using tins that are the same size (diameter) but different styles, weigh your mixture in the mixer bowl and then divide it among your tins.
- **MIXER BOWL WEIGHT**—weigh your mixer bowl when it's empty and make a note of the weight. I have actually scratched the weight onto the side of each metal mixer bowl in my kitchen; that way I never lose the thing I wrote it down on. When you want to know how much mixture you have, just put the full mixer bowl on the scales and subtract the scratched-on weight. TA-DA!
- **AVOIDING A DOME ON YOUR CAKE**—lay a clean tea towel over the top of the cake as soon as you remove it from the oven, and press down firmly on the dome to flatten it out. Trust me, this does not damage the cake and will do away with that pesky dome.
- **BUTTERCREAMS**—I hear that many people encounter issues with air bubbles in their Swiss, Italian, German and French buttercreams. If you are using your buttercream fresh from the mixer, I recommend switching from your whisk attachment after your buttercream is made and replacing it with the beater attachment. Set your mixer to low speed, and leave it mixing slowly for about 5 mins. This will greatly reduce the air-bubble situation. If the buttercream is already on the

cake and you're doing the scrapy-scrape with your Magnolia Kitchen sharp-as-shit scraper and you're getting those pesky drag marks and air bubbles, DON'T STRESS. It simply means that your buttercream is too cold. Either the room you are working in is too cold, or the chilled cake is cooling your icing too fast while you are working. To counteract this, simply put your buttercream in the microwave for 10-second bursts, stirring well between bursts until a soft, smooth consistency is reached. Personally, in winter I prefer to overcompensate for the chill in the air by softening slightly more than usual so that I have a chance to get to the scraping point comfortably before the buttercream hardens.

- **COLOURING CHOCOLATE**—ALWAYS use powdered food colour or oil-based food colour. If using powdered colour, melt the required amount of chocolate. Separate off one-third of your melted chocolate and add the powdered colour until the chocolate is at least two shades darker than required. Mix the powder in well, until the chocolate starts to go thick and set. Re-heat until melted and add to the remaining melted chocolate. I have found that this technique ensures a uniform colour with no specks or lumps of colour.
- **FOOD COLOUR**—gel food colours are the best to work with in baking and icings, including ganache. They are thicker and won't disrupt the consistency.
- **CAKE PAINTING**—obviously this is something I do a lot. I love painting with the edible art paints made by Sweet Sticks. I will also use petal dusts mixed with rose spirit. I use these to paint on both ganache and royal icing. If I am needing to 'paint' on a buttercream cake, I will go with a design that is more textured and use softened coloured buttercream.
- **SHELF LIVES**—usually when I get asked about this, my rule-of-thumb answer is 'if it's got mould, it's past its use-by date'. The fact is, when things are made at home and I'm not there it is hard to give an answer better than that. Store your caramels, curds and compotes in the fridge. Always use a clean utensil when you are working with them—don't double-dip or cross-contaminate. But the logic still stands: if it's got mould or smells funny, don't eat it.
- **MAKING CAKES AHEAD OF TIME**—you do not need to be superhuman and bake and ice your cake all in one day. If you are busy, I recommend spacing it out. For example, if your event is on a Saturday then bake on Wednesday, and ice and decorate on Thursday. Friday is for emergencies or extended decorating. Saturday is the no-stress event. Think of your icing being like an airtight container—the sooner you ice your cake, the better it can be stored until you eat it. An iced cake can last upwards of one week when stored in the fridge; bring it to room temperature before eating. You can also freeze individual layers of baked cake for up to six months. All of my cakes defrost to room temp with no change to the texture or quality. You can

BOARDS

also freeze leftovers with the same results. Simply defrost in the fridge before icing your cake. If you are defrosting to consume it, bring it to room temp for the best eating experience.

INGREDIENT TIPS

As I said in my first book, I have spent countless hours and probably an exorbitant amount of money working with shit ingredients, so I know the good stuff when I find it. Trust me on these.

- **BUTTER**—salted always.
- **DAIRY-FREE BUTTER SUBSTITUTE**—Olivani. You can use this to substitute for butter in all of my recipes.
- **GOOD-QUALITY COCOA—**Dutch cocoa or Valrhona 100% cocoa.
- **EGGS**—any size. If a recipe says '1 egg' then use one egg. For egg whites, weigh them as you would any liquid. An egg yolk is an egg yolk and should be counted as one egg yolk. Unless of course it is a double-yolker, then it should be counted as two.
- **EGG-FREE SUBSTITUTE**—aquafaba, which is the viscous water that chickpeas have been cooked in, and comes in the can with them. It mimics the properties of egg white, so can be used as a substitute where a recipe specifies egg white. When it comes to vegan baking, Bruce is your man—he 'invented' aquafaba, didn't you know, and is affectionately referred to as the Messiah! If you haven't yet been introduced to Bruce, you are missing out. I chat about him in my first book and he does make an appearance in this book. He is a bloody intelligent cool dude, not to be underestimated! (Disclaimer: Bruce is not real and he did not invent aquafaba. In reality he is my alter-ego fictional character . . . I have gone so far as to create a whole fictional life for him with a girlfriend/love story, and he even has friends that I have named!)
- **FLOUR**—yes, I know there are literally *hundreds* of types of flour, but when I say 'flour' or 'plain flour' that is *exactly* what I mean. Basic-ass plain ole white flour. NOT self-raising flour. NOT cake flour. NOT high-grade flour. NOT bread flour. JUST FLOUR—PLAIN. If I do call for any other type of flour, trust that I will specify it in the recipe.
- **CORNFLOUR**—in New Zealand this is what we call cornstarch.
- **GLUTEN-FREE FLOUR**—I use a pre-mix that is made up of tapioca starch, rice flour and thickeners. Gluten-free flour can be used in my recipes as a direct 1:1 substitute.
- **VANILLA BEAN PASTE**—Equagold. This stuff is AMAZING, it is super-quality and worth every cent. Whatever brand you are using, it pays to check the details on the packet to make sure it's the real deal.
- **FLAVOURS AND OILS**—LorAnn. You can buy their products at most cake-supply stores around the world. The natural oils are amazing, the citrus oils too, and of course I love their cream cheese flavour!

TOOLS

These are just some of the tools I love to use when creating cake designs. I try not to limit myself to 'cake' tools or tools that are specifically designed for baking and decorating. As with designing, I prefer to think more outside the box. This is how I came up with most of my range of cake tools that we sell at Magnolia Kitchen.

Often when I am creating a cake I find myself thinking, *What could I use to create this look?* and I search for something that works. I then quickly realise that this 'something that works' is a valuable tool for cake design in the Magnolia Kitchen studio and range.

If you are looking for inspiration to create new designs, I have had huge success with art tools. Just remember: it needs to be new and it needs to become a dedicated food/cake tool. This will avoid cross-contamination.

1. *Flower Colour Guide* by Darroch and Michael Putnam
2. Paint palette
3. Lace samples
4. Edible art paint by Sweet Sticks
5. 'Metallic Lustre' by Sweet Sticks
6. Paint brushes, various sizes
7. Magnolia Kitchen watercolour brush
8. Rose spirit
9. Dropper
10. Magnolia Kitchen mini metal scraper
11. Sponges
12. Magnolia Kitchen palette knife
13. Printed illustration

I've listed the book *Flower Colour Guide* (published by Phaidon Press, 2018) here as it gives a great insight into the different flowers you can use as colour and type references for drawings and fresh florals on cakes. For me, painting flowers and using pictures of them as inspiration for art is my favourite pastime. Back when I used to paint on canvas, in my life before cake art, I would spend a lot of time at the library finding nature books, flower books and gardening books with images that I could use on my canvas. You could always use Google, but nothing beats holding an image in your hands. Better yet, get out there and take images yourself!

The edible art paints I love to use for painting on cakes are by my talented friend Miranda of Sweet Sticks. She and I met online when our businesses were so teeny tiny and only a glimmer in our eyes. Both of us have hustled our way to where we are today, and it was with pride in 2020 that Miranda and I collaborated to create some specific Magnolia Kitchen colours. You can now get 'Magnolia'—a beautiful magenta burgundy reminiscent of the beautiful Japanese magnolia; 'Moss Green'—what I think of as 'dirty' green, that perfect winter colour which reminds me of the magnolia bud right before the beauty emerges (mix it with a touch of white to give that furry look the bud has, or use it to accent wood as a true moss); and 'Antique Gold'—a beautiful rich gold that reminds me of a gilt frame you would see in an art gallery or a museum. (Tip: you can mix 'Moss Green' with 'Magnolia' for a warm brown.)

As you can see, I have gone with two tool pages for this book. Not only because, shit, there are just *so many* 'go to' designing tools to share with you guys, but also because the images of all the tools scattered around are just too beautiful and it seemed unfair to only have one. And yep, some of these tools appear twice, but that's because they're so important.

1. Magnolia Kitchen turntable
2. Cake board
3. Double-sided tape
4. Fresh flowers
5. Dried flowers
6. Florist wire
7. Exacto knife
8. Screwdriver
9. Screw
10. 2 mm diameter dowel
11. Hand saw
12. Secateurs
13. Magnolia Kitchen mini metal scraper
14. Smoothie straws
15. Magnolia Kitchen palette knife
16. Craft snips
17. Magnolia Kitchen sharp-as-shit scraper
18. Florist tape

Now there are plenty of tools I'll mention in the book that aren't in these pictures, and that is simply because it was impossible to remember everything and also fit them all in. I have taken care to list the required tools in each step-by-step, so make sure you read the tools list there before starting.

Please don't take any of these lists as gospel—if you don't have a tool that I've listed, don't go crazy trying to find it. Just wing it and find something that works. (Unless it's a Magnolia Kitchen tool, then I'm sorry but that is a must—there is no replacement for the greatness of these tools, honest. Okay SALES PITCH, but seriously I have carefully selected these tools before putting my name on them and I rate the fuck out of them.)

MAGNOLIA KITCHEN RANGE

- *Magnolia Kitchen: Inspired Baking with Personality*
- Magnolia Kitchen turntable
- Sharp-as-shit scrapers duo
- Big Daddy scraper
- Mini metal scraper set
- Acrylic disk set
- Decorating watercolour brushes
- Cake detailing palette knife set
- Icing spatula set
- Edible art paint collaboration
- Magnolia Kitchen apron
- Reusable cold drink cup
- Luxe soy candle
- Reusable hot drink cup
- 16 online courses

MY JOURNEY
OF INSPIRATION

—

INSPIRATION
/ˌɪnspɪˈreɪʃ(ə)n/

noun

1. the process of being mentally stimulated to do or feel something, especially to do something creative.

'Bets had one of her flashes of inspiration.'

Similar: creativity, inventiveness, innovation, innovativeness, ingenuity, imagination, imaginativeness, originality, individuality, artistry, expressiveness, creative power, creative talent, creative skill, genius, insight, vision, wit, finesse, flair, brilliance, sophistication

2. a sudden brilliant or timely idea.

'Then I had an inspiration.'

from Lexico.com, published by Oxford University Press, 2019; see lexico.com/en/definition/inspiration (Did you spot the tweak?)

————

What makes me tick? I am often asked what inspires me, how I come up with ideas and designs. I wanted to try to get this down on paper, though really there is no formula for inspiration. To feel inspired by something is such an individual, personal thing that it's hard to think it can be taught.

It can be easy to feel confined by comfort zones, or by customers, or by what you identify as being 'good at'. Customers often choose from examples of our work online, almost like choosing from a catalogue, and it's hard being given your own design from two years ago and asked to re-create it! Personally, I get bored of designs and techniques over time and feel that if I am re-creating I'm not *creating*. This may or may not be true, but it's how my stubborn creative brain sees things!

My hope in creating this book is that I can describe not only the techniques but also my process . . . and thus inspire individuality and trust in your imagination and your ability to create.

My 'go to' places for inspiration are nature, buildings, fashion and art—there is so much that can be used to create beautiful designs.

Flowers of course are where I feel most at home. They make me happy: smelling them, feeling them, receiving them, seeing them in the wild, putting them on cake, drawing them—I mean, what is not to love? I have mentioned before that I love nature's penchant for imperfection—two flowers never bloom exactly the same, and an unfurled petal can be what makes a specific flower seem unique and special. Rose petals can tear and fold, and that adds to their beauty. This is why I love working with flowers, not just real flowers and dried flowers but painted ones too. There is a feeling of freedom in drawing or painting a flower; it was never meant to be perfect, so why try to replicate something that was always supposed to be a one-off?

Don't get me wrong—I forget this all the time and get super fucked-off when my rose looks like a mutant hand-puppet instead of a perfect rose. When this happens, I always go back to *loosely* basing the design on the original. If I keep that in mind, I am going to work harder to make it individual.

The best thing is that if someone was ever to say, 'Oh, that doesn't look like a flower', you can feel confident that their imagination just isn't like yours. Your art and design is defined by what you create, not by what they see. I always think of art critics and how odd that job title is. Like, why do *they* get to say what is or isn't 'good' or 'great' art? Creating and viewing art is such an individual thing, and yes, not everyone will like it but that is okay because art is interpretive.

Anyway, that is just my little way of reminding myself to care less about perfection!

Nature is the gift that keeps on giving. Think textures of bark on a kauri tree . . . layers of reds and browns almost like patchwork, and sometimes grey moss. How cool would that look on a cake? If you're not from New Zealand where the kauri is a native tree you might not be familiar with it, but there are other cool trees to inspire: Korean stewartia, kousa dogwood, lacebark elm . . . Have I mentioned that I love trees? The beach is also a treasure trove: the rocks on the shore, lines of sediment in the cliffs as you walk around the rocks, waving grasses hanging off the side of a cliff, shells and pebbles . . .

Buildings are a never-ending supply of inspiration, designed by an architect as their own expression of art. I love the textures of the different materials, the lines of the bricks, stone blocks and windows, the shadows they create as the sun hits them.

Art has been my biggest inspiration for technique for a while now. I actually had a purge of my Instagram a while back, choosing to curate my feed with fewer completed cakes and more raw materials to give inspiration. I didn't want to feel like I was constantly looking at someone else's cake designs, so I started following a huge number of artists, sculptors, ceramicists, potters, fashion designers, florists, interior designers and architects. It was so refreshing to see an artist creating a watercolour and find myself thinking 'Ohhhhh, that style or technique would look incredible on a cake.' That textured oil paint would look *amazing* as an abstract textured design using coloured ganache . . . the colour combinations and the directions of the brush strokes. Even simple line illustrations have the power to inspire me to not be constrained by what is specific to food design and cake design. Why shouldn't I use ceramic scrapers as cake tools? Why shouldn't I use watercolour reservoir brushes and colours mixed with rose spirit to paint on cakes? Why shouldn't I repurpose oil-paint palette knives as Magnolia Kitchen cake detailing palette knives?

The same goes for fashion, textures, edgy designs, colour blocking, movement—it all inspires design. Why should one particular inspiration be used just for fashion? Enter my favourite saying: 'food fashion'. Just like with the fashion we wear, there are trends, designs that are used across the world, materials, looks and styles. (Let us not forget the unicorn cake haha.)

I guess to bring it to a point: individuality in design is so important to me. What inspires me may not inspire you, and that is okay. Open your mind to the possibilities, look outside your industry, and don't fall into the trap of thinking that design and inspiration have to mean perfection.

THE MAGNOLIA

This cake design was planned from the moment I saw an artwork in an art shop in Kyoto, Japan, where I was holidaying with Harley and Charlotte in October 2019. My obsession with the magnolia flower lives on!

Everywhere I went in Japan, it had become a habit to ask if they had any art, fans, ceramics or other items with magnolias on them. The joy I felt when the shop owner nodded and then presented me with a completely stunning magnolia 'woodcut' print was almost overwhelming. I immediately fell in love with this beautiful piece of art and knew I had to use it in a cake design. After all, we *are* Magnolia Kitchen—even though by this time Harley and Charlotte had realised I was on a mission and had gone off to check out other shops.

Of course I bought the print.

There was an info sheet in the sleeve behind the picture, but unfortunately the only English was 'Magnolia grandiflora', 'North carolina' (with a small 'c') and 'Texas'. I believe it gives a descriptive background on the type of magnolia depicted in the print. I did try to use Google Translate, but to be honest it wasn't helpful—though I'll let y'all decide . . .

> *To be sexually friendly water, in South America of North Carolina Texas. It's a land of trolls and grand Den Clen.*
>
> *The water god is flaming after many school work and forms an external triangle.*
>
> *Considering the objective shape, the length of the Imperial Army is divided into 6 dimensions and it is of full-grade thick hardness . . .*

I'm sorry, I can't stop laughing at the full-grade thick hardness!!

I was curious about the technique used to create the print. The print came in a beautiful olive-green paper sleeve, and the paper it is printed on is a beautiful vintage yellow-ivory colour. The shades of the magnolia and the leaves look stunning on the paper. If I run my finger over the picture I can feel ridges where the outlines of the flower and the leaves are. So away I went on a Google tangent to discover all I could about 'woodcuts'. I now believe this is probably a mistranslation, as the technique is actually called 'woodblock printing', and let me tell you IT BLEW MY MIND!!

(This is why I love art and love the inspiration and awe that comes with it.) The woodblock printing technique originated in China and came to Japan before the 1500s. It was originally used for printing, but later became a style of art. The process involves carving negative space out of wood to depict images and then using these to stamp colours onto fabric or paper laid on top, with the stamping repeated to create layers of colours on the finished print. The indents that I could feel were created when the paper was pressed onto the wooden carving. Trust me, there is so much to discover about this technique—just researching it has sparked further inspiration and ideas for future designs.

There isn't much of a mood board for this cake other than the colour scheme and the original print, because the design process was very cut and dried from print to cake. Usually I would use art just to inspire my own designs, but on this occasion I didn't want to mess with the perfection of the magnolia print. So I decided to freehand draw and paint the exact(ish) magnolia onto the cake in a semi-washed-out watercolour style.

I do love the memories that this magnolia print and the subsequent cake design hold for my time with my family in Japan.

The Magnolia

- Ivory ganache finish with raw-textured edges

- Japanese wood block magnolia print hand-painted accross two tiers

Top tier: 6×6 inch round.
Bottom tier: 8×6 inch round

DESIGN DEBRIEF
I have nothing to say about this cake other than YOU COMPLETE ME.
I wouldn't change a single thing—from concept to completion it is exactly
as I imagined for the design.

FLORAL ABSTRACT WEDDING

Normally I try not to take any cake design orders in December, as it is our busiest month for online orders and the cafe due to Christmas. That said, I always end up with some wedding orders—I can't help it. I feel that spark of creativity right from the initial contact.

Libby and Arnold were getting married in early December 2019 at Abbeville Estate in south Auckland, and upon hearing Libby's ideas for their cake I immediately knew I had to book in this wedding. They were unsure of the size required and were open to being creatively led by me—dream customers right there! The colour scheme for the wedding was white and dusky pinks, and they requested that the cake flowers match the wedding flowers. Libby provided some inspiration images with elements of cakes they liked, and guess what? These were all previous designs I had completed—which was great, as I got to use my own work as visual inspiration, and it made the mood board even more epic because it's filled with past Magnolia Kitchen works.

One of the cakes Libby liked was a square, concrete-style cake. Straight away I knew I wanted to work with an abstract style as a base, then bring in some softer aspects to the design with the dusky pink and florals.

Instead of a grey concrete look, I decided to make it more of a white stone style which would be in keeping with the colours of the wedding. And in keeping with the abstract theme and to create more flow with the design, I suggested incorporating chocolate sculptures—I felt that these would give a great edgy feel in contrast to the florals and pinks.

Libby also sent through a lot of floral inspiration images so I could get a good idea of the flowers she was aiming to have in her wedding. This sort of thing helps me to sketch up the concept, as it lets me think about the larger flowers and the fillers that I will likely be using as part of the design on the day. The florist for the big day was Ruby Rose Flower Studio in Parnell, whose team does incredible work. As I've said before, I always have the wedding florist for the day provide the cake florals so that they match with the whole event, and then I add these to the cake on-site. It's one of my favourite things to do!

My initial design concept read as follows:
- *2 tiers, 8-inch square, 4-inch square + 4-inch round*
- *Approx. 40 dessert serves or 80 coffee serves*

The 8-inch square will be the structure for the design. On top will sit the 4-inch square, positioned on one corner of the bottom tier. The round 4-inch cake will be positioned at the centre of the bottom tier, touching the middle corner of the 4-inch square. All tiers to be covered with white chocolate ganache in a stone look, with raw-textured edges around the top. All will feature dusky pink highlights in oil-paint style, with fresh florals and chocolate sculptures to create more height and flow.

Libby and Arnold discussed the design, and decided that they would like to go larger with the cake. They were entirely happy with the concept, so I just adjusted the sizes while maintaining the basic design. Adding another small round cake on the top as a third tier enhanced the overall drama of the cake. Some of the inspo designs Libby had chosen also featured gold leaf, so I incorporated that into the revised design as well.

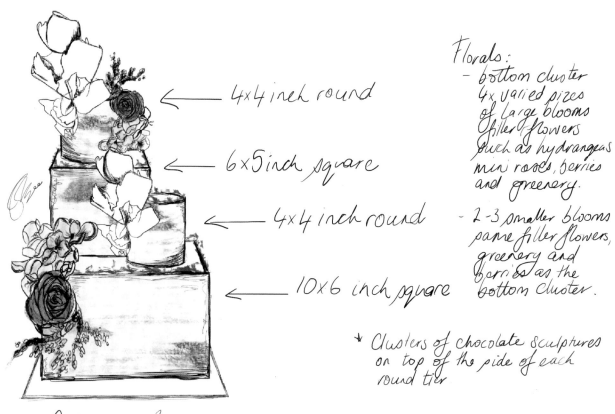

4x4 inch round

6x5 inch square

4x4 inch round

10x6 inch square

Florals:
- bottom cluster
  4x varied sizes
  of large blooms
  filler flowers
  such as hydrangeas
  mini roses, berries
  and greenery.

- 2-3 smaller blooms
  same filler flowers,
  greenery and
  berries as the
  bottom cluster.

* Clusters of chocolate sculptures
  on top of the side of each
  round tier

Cake Finish: ivory chocolate ganache in
stone look with raw-textured edges.
Dusty pink oil-paint features layered with
touches of gold leaf

PAINTED BIRD DESIGN

A couple of years ago I was inspired by a piece of art and used it to create a cake, and within this design was a bird (it's pictured in the mood board). I love birds—I love watching them and imagining what it would be like to be one . . . it seems so free to be able to fly places, to see the world from such a high vantage point. It seems so safe. I definitely hope I spend another life as a bird!!

Anyway . . . ever since I painted that bird on the cake I have been itching to create more bird art. I got the opportunity to do a fantail piece in late 2019 at the Hannah Jensen workshop I attended in Christchurch. There was no cake involved and actually not really any painting—or at least not detail painting. Hannah's art is comprised of multiple layers of paint over a wooden board—I'm talking 50+ layers!! Then she sketches a quick design on the dry paint layers and uses a carving tool to carve into the layers and create this amazing texture and art. (Side note: Hannah is amazing, and if you want to be inspired go and check out her work. She is also the most epic human and I just love listening to her Instagram stories. She starts every day with 'Good morning beautiful humans' in the most sing-song, calming way.)

Obviously I'd thought I would do a flower at the workshop, but as we were researching images I remembered the bird on the cake. I picked a beautiful piwakawaka (fantail) image and used this to sketch and then carve onto my board in Hannah's style (my creation is shown in the mood board, bottom left). It further inspired what is now a deep need to create more bird art, but this time on cakes.

For this design I wanted a smaller two-tier cake, to keep it delicate. I would make it slightly ethereal by using a blush-coloured textured ganache finish over the whole cake. I do love piwakawaka so I decided to sketch some of these into the design. We get these cheeky birds out in our native bush, and they flit around from branch to branch and often follow you for a while along a bush walk.

For the colour scheme I chose to go with browns and yellows. The first step would be to wash out the background with a light watercolour, then sketch the bird in basic lines over the top, with maybe a small amount of shading to give detail. This design would work really well with some flowers added among the birds; actually, my tattoo artist Triton Ly does incredible floral bird work, and his work is another huge inspiration for me.

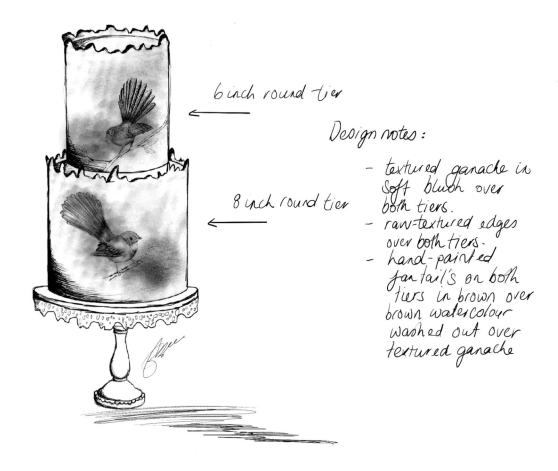

6 inch round tier

Design notes:

- textured ganache in soft blush over both tiers.
- raw-textured edges over both tiers.
- hand-painted fantail's on both tiers in brown over brown watercolour washed out over textured ganache

8 inch round tier

DESIGN DEBRIEF

Best-laid plans . . . the cheeky piwakawaka was elusive to me, so without a proper inspiration image for reference I started thinking further outside the box. I stumbled across these printed Hobbytex place-setting cloths that depicted a bird sitting on a blossom branch! Epic—this was now the direction I wanted to go in.

I stayed loosely with my original design, which was the textured light blush with the painting of a bird. I dropped the yellow colour and just used a single shade of brown. I switched between watercolour, lines and layering to give the painting life. Originally, as per my sketch, I had wanted two birds. When I'd finished the bird on the bottom tier, however, I'll be honest—I got bored with the bird and didn't want to paint another. Instead, I pieced together branches and blossoms from the various images to create the illustration on the second tier.

I love the finished product so much, and I think this is a great representation of letting the design remain loose and letting it lead you. If I had remained rigid about following the original description—or even my sketch—I wouldn't have come away happy. I am forever grateful to have customers who allow me this kind of creativity.

PATTERNED TILE DESIGN

Let's chat Instagram—a wealth of inspiration, am I right?!

I recently started following a custom tile company, which posts videos of their team painting tiles. It is so epic to watch—the designs and lines are incredibly inspiring. (If you want to check them out, they are @fireclaytile . . . the videos are so satisfying!!)

Once I focus on something that inspires me, I start to notice it everywhere I go. I had been planning a tile design for a while, just waiting for the right tile inspiration and customer that I could convince to let me create it for them. I actually did a Spanish blocking tile design a while back for a styled shoot. It was this vibrant deep blue and white and the design went straight up the middle of the cake. The tiers went blue, white, blue and the tiles were opposite colours to the tier—so the blue tiers had white tiles and white tier had blue tiles.

But back to the current cake. I saw these tiles at a cafe in Mount Maunganui called Eddies and Elspeth. Of course I was that weirdo crouching down at the counter taking photos of their tiles. I have no shame anymore when it comes to inspiration and taking photos! As you can see in the mood board, the tiles are a mixture of charcoal, light blue and off-white. If you single out one tile it has four corners to it, with the design in each corner matching up to the design on the next tile.

My plan was to single out one full design, centred on one tile, rather than piecing the tile corners together as they have done here. To me it looks like there are two designs here, and I wanted to focus on just one . . . I wanted each tile to be a stand-alone.

Having singled out my tile design, I asked my friends at Peg Creative to make me a stencil out of thin plastic, which they can laser-cut with their fancy machines. I could then use the stencils with ganache to transfer the tile design onto the cake.

My initial plan was that the pattern would be a line of tiles ringing the middle of each tier. Once I had stencilled the design onto the cake, I wanted to paint each tile design in a gold metallic paint. The rest of the finish for the cake would be a textured stone in white/ivory.

I wasn't sure whether I wanted to add flowers to this cake; sometimes I need to stand back and look at the design before I know if it needs the addition of something more. I was thinking that if I did choose to do flowers I would use some preserved roses. I already had a box of freeze-dried roses that I got from Simply Roses in Australia, in a beautiful ivory colour. I bought them on a whim, not knowing what I would use them for.

As soon as I remembered those flowers I decided that they must be incorporated into the design. The tricky decision would be placement. Maybe something a little different, and have them sitting on the front edge of each tier . . . You will have to skip ahead to the finished design to see what I decided to do, as even I didn't know until it came to the day.

- basic cream natural white chocolate ganache over all tiers

- detailed tile stencils evenly around the the centre of each tier in white chocolate ganache

- I want the tile stencil to be subtle against the cream coloured ganache.

- secondary design would be to paint the stencilling gold.

I think definitely include flowers now that I have drawn them on undecided on the floral placement?? will make a judgement call once a real cake

top tier 5 inch
middle tier 7 inch
bottom tier 9 inch

* all tiers approx. 5 inches tall

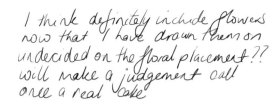

DESIGN DEBRIEF

Another favourite: classic and old-fashioned, but not in a cringe way. Romantic but a little edgy. It isn't at all what I intended for it, though— which is typical of what I do when I design. I do stay true to the base guidelines. I've used the tiles, although I knew after I sketched the cake that they would work better around the top of each tier. Instead of having textured ganache I've kept it smooth and sharp-as-shit. I don't feel like this was a conscious decision . . . maybe it was an accident or an oversight? Anyway, it was a happy change in the design as I think it offsets the raised tile pattern perfectly.

I did try to paint the tile pattern with gold but abandoned that idea when I fell in love with the subtleness of the tile pattern on its own. The roses, though. Oh my, the roses! Something about the colour of them just felt right against the ganache. I went for my classic diagonal arrangement, but kept it off-centre so as not to dominate the subtle tile design. As I was placing the roses, some of the petals fluttered down, and one petal caught on the edge of the ganached tile. As I looked at it, sitting there separate from the cluster, I took its lead and added more separate petals at random. I even made use of the empty buds with just the stamens showing. This cake was such a process, and I almost felt like it appeared in front of me complete. IN LOVE.

FRENCH SKETCH DESIGN

So . . . my daughter Charlotte is as arty as fuck! I'm often jealous of her talent . . . it's okay to be jealous of your child, right? It's a compliment, right? Charlotte draws, illustrates and paints, and experiments with loads of different mediums. This makes her easy to buy presents for—she can always use an art-shop gift card to keep her supplies topped up. Her bedroom is filled with art she has created, some of it half-finished (which usually means she has lost her shit because it didn't look how she wanted it to . . . I don't know where she gets that from, honestly). She does my head in as she often leaves wet paint palettes on her workbench, and we wake up in the morning to find painted cat pawprints leading from her desk and out of her room into the lounge. Luckily her paint of choice is acrylic and not oil!!

This lovely Charlotte tangent I have gone off on is leading somewhere, don't worry. Charlotte's friends obviously know her well too—one of her friends was in Paris (pre-Covid-19) and bought her this gorgeous artwork. I instantly imagined a canal in summer with loads of artists creating art alongside it, selling their wares. I actually have no idea if this correct, but I prefer to imagine it this way so no one is allowed to correct me. And the more I look at the picture, the more the scene makes me feel this way.

As soon as Charlotte showed me the drawing I knew I wanted to use it as inspiration for a cake. It just feels so romantic—I know this is cliché Paris vibes but I just *love* the washed-out watercolour, with the lines depicting old stone buildings and (I imagine) cobblestoned streets. I love that the lines are just a hint and not perfect, just enough to give you a feeling for the scene . . . almost encouraging you to fill in the blanks. I've decided it is spring too—the colours the artist used give me the impression that the trees are in blossom.

I decided to stay quite true to the painting, so I chose an ivory ganache base, with raw-textured edges to echo the slightly rough paper the scene is painted on. Then watercolour in grey and violet pinky-purple, finished with black lines. The sketch would be depicted over one extra-tall tier and kept to the front of the cake. I wanted to add some fresh stock flowers to it in some way too, although the actual arrangement would only be decided when I had finished the painting and could see what would work best. I didn't want it to be heavy with greenery; I wanted to keep the colour scheme of the flowers and the romantic feel simple, by using the stock. Bonus too—it smells INCREDIBLE.

345

5. Pl. du Tertre.
aquarelle

Extra tall tier in textured stone-look ganache. Ivory colour

raw-textured edges

Small fresh flowers in similar colours to the painting. long stemmed to create yet more height

watercolour style with sketch in black over the top.

DESIGN DEBRIEF

I always wanted to stay true to the original sketch of this scene, keeping it very impressionistic, with the watercolour and outlines giving the feeling of France rather than focusing on the perfection of how the scene should look.

Although I wanted to use fresh stock flowers, I was inspired by the colour of the lilac which is shown in the mood board. As I was sketching the design, I started to worry about how these flowers were going to look in among the art, placed against the cake. So I changed the design slightly, and chose to go for height with a delicate spray of pink dried flowers—it worked perfectly to further elongate the cake and give a more elegant look to the overall design.

ACRYLIC BOX DESIGN

Oh to be in my head … I will try to do justice to my imagination when talking about this design. It had been sitting around in my head for over a year! I wanted this cake to be the ultimate showstopper, to be remembered—there would be gasps when people first saw it and then *oohs* and *ahhs* as they closed in to see the detail. I imagined people would even take selfies with it … or am I the only one who takes selfies with cakes? Haha.

In my imagination the cake was being displayed in the centre of the room with the dining tables surrounding it, like you would display an ice sculpture. Look, I *know* that the wedding isn't about the cake (I say this, but isn't it?). The guests are there to witness a display of love between the happy couple, but I mean—it's cake art. Can we just pretend it's the centre of attention just for this design?

Throughout my career in the wedding industry I have seen trends come and go. Some come back, and some I hope remain gone. One that has been used by florists over the past couple of seasons has been acrylic plinths filled with floral displays, and they are incredible! Such an inspiring way to display flowers. It truly makes me think of the forbidden rose in *Beauty and the Beast*. It feels romantic and untouchable at the same time. I started to wonder, as I often do when I home in on a design or a look I love, how I could incorporate this into a cake design. Of course flowers are a no-brainer for a cake design, but an acrylic plinth? Then I remembered: years and years ago I had some PVC cylinders made to send out Mother's Day cakes in. The cakes looked SO beautiful displayed in them. Obviously, though, I wouldn't want to lock away a HUGE FOUR-TIER WEDDING CAKE inside an acrylic plinth!

Then it hit me: why not create a fake tier out of acrylic?! GENIUS. The idea that I could create something non-edible to incorporate into the structure of the cake was an instant hit, and had my creativity bursting. The lines of the acrylic would work perfectly as a square, and the sharp-as-shit edges would tie in perfectly with my branding (which as we know is heavily 'sharp-as-shit').

I decided that for this project it would be a lot easier to make a square acrylic box the right size. So I got my friends at Peg Creative to cut me flat pieces of acrylic that were 20 cm (8 in) square. These I would glue together into a cube, leaving the bottom open.

The full size of the cake had to be four tiers so that there would be three tiers of cake for the guests to eat, with the acrylic tier obviously just for show.

I wanted the entire cake to be ivory and sharp-as-shit on every edge, to match the perfection of the acrylic box. The box would be filled with an array of fresh blooms, to feel like beauty locked away. It would sit on top of a 10-inch square cake, then have a 6-inch and a 5-inch on top. I planned to use more florals on the cake, and have these move up from the acrylic box onto the middle-top tier as if they were escaping the confines of the box. Yeah, and they'd escape down onto the bottom tier too.

Using gold paint I would also illustrate a few flowers peeking out from behind the fresh florals . . . to soften and romanticise the design slightly, and to offset the sharpness of the square tiers.

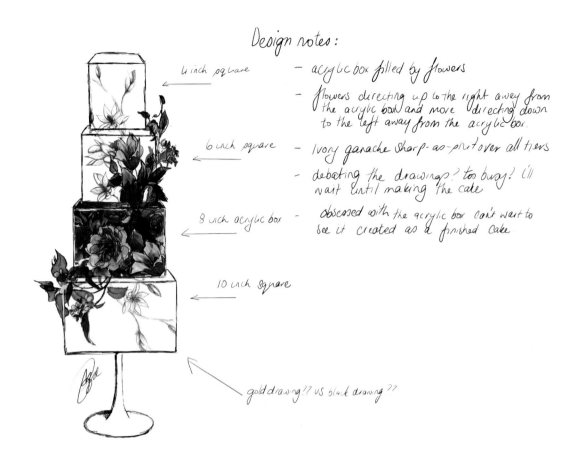

Design notes:

4 inch square → — acrylic box filled by flowers
— flowers directing up to the right away from the acrylic box and more directing down to the left away from the acrylic box.

6 inch square → — Ivory ganache sharp-as-phit over all tiers
— debating the drawings? too busy? I'll wait until making the cake

8 inch acrylic box → — obsessed with the acrylic box can't wait to see it created as a finished cake.

10 inch square →

← gold drawing?? vs black drawing??

DESIGN DEBRIEF

From original concept to completed physical design . . . originally I wanted to add hand-painting to this design. In my design inspiration I thought this might add a softness to the sharp edges and the restricting feel of the acrylic box.

When I got to the actual construction of the cake, I remember adding each fresh bloom 'escaping' from the acrylic and then stepping back, assessing, then adding another bloom, and so on. By the time I had added the florals and was happy with the direction, I took one final step back and knew that I had achieved showstopper status without needing any painting.

It's so important to allow this freedom within the design; to know when to stop. This isn't often my forte (more is usually more, haha), but I'm really happy with this balance of fresh romantic flowers against the contrasting sharpness of the rest of the cake.

PAINTED HUNTING WEDDING

It all started with an email enquiry, of course . . . Angela (the bride-to-be) mentioned in her comments: 'If possible, art comprising deer and ducks as my partner is a huge fan of hunting.' I absolutely *love* that the groom was being included in the design for the cake—though I will admit that initially I was like 'how the fuck am I going to incorporate hunting into the design?' It's not your classic or typical vibe for a wedding cake, right? But I also absolutely love a challenge.

Angela and I had a few back-and-forth emails so that I could find out a bit more about her and her fiancé Douglas and also get a feel for the wedding planning, colour scheme, venue, florals, etc. Here's the info Angela sent through:

> *Things that inspire . . .*
> - *Venue: the venue is an old restored woolshed, with a very rustic country vibe*
> - *Florals: whites and greenery*
> - *Colour schemes: bridesmaids will be in navy, will be doing basic navy/gold*
> - *Likes and dislikes of the couple: dislike bright pinks, bride loves Disney and baking, partner loves hunting (duck and deer)*
> - *Stationery: very minimal, invites are black with gold*
> - *Theme: classic, white and gold, moody, rustic, country*

From the list of inspos the points that really jumped out to trigger my creativity were Disney and hunting—this immediately made me think of Gaston from *Beauty and the Beast*, of course; it's my all-time favourite Disney movie (if you know, you know). I had this image in my head of Gaston shooting some ducks and a depiction of a forest landscape painting. I didn't want to make it exact, of course—more of an ode to a hunting scene. Not focused on hunting and not focused on Gaston specifically, but just using those points as inspiration.

Here is my initial design and concept:
- *2 tiers, both round, 8 inches and 6 inches*
- *Approx. 40 dessert serves or 80 coffee serves*

Ivory white chocolate ganache over both tiers with raw-textured edges around the top. Hand-painted design around bottom tier in navy blue lines and watercolour look, depicting a forest landscape scene with a hint at hunting—nothing too obvious, perhaps just the outline of a man with a gun and some ducks flying in the distance (Angela—think Gaston hehe). The art will be vague, only a sketch of lines overlaying watercolour and touches of gold leaf. The top tier will mostly be left simple and white with touches of gold leaf. Topped with fresh greenery to match the wedding florals.

There were a few emails back and forth after this, but in the end we settled on the original concept; the final things to lock in were the delivery info and the cake flavours. Angela and Douglas went with lemon cake with lemon curd and white chocolate ganache for one tier, and raspberry and white chocolate ganache for the other tier.

I like to give an idea of design but not be constrained by it. When I actually have the cake in front of me *that* is when the creativity really flows. You can see, going from written design to sketch to the finished product, how much an idea can grow and take on a life of its own. Embrace the process and be inspired.

Design details: ivory ganache finish with raw-textured edges

hand-painting predominantly on the bottom tier and moving
slightly up to the top tier to give direction.
painting style to be vague with a landscape feel
but also water colour.
Accent painting with touches of gold leaf.

earthy colours

6 inch

8 inch

florals provided by wedding
florist.
— whites and greens
— arranged
from the top of
the cake and
flowing down
one side

DRIED HYDRANGEA DESIGN

Dried hydrangeas are a thing of beauty. They are like delicate butterflies tied together into perfect bunches.

When I made the decision to relocate Magnolia Kitchen (you can read about this at the beginning of the book), I knew I needed to add more cloud lights from Richard Clarkson Studio, as these lights have become synonymous with my cafe interior. That said, the ceilings in the new space were HUGE . . . I knew that I wasn't going to be able to fill the ceiling with clouds so I decided to include hydrangea clouds.

My friend Sharon, who runs Matui Honey with her husband Dan and also supplies flowers and greenery to the wholesale flower markets, has the most *incredible* collection of hydrangea bushes. I knew from past conversations with Sharon that the best dried hydrangeas are blooms that have been left on the bush for some time. I think they are called vintage hydrangeas. They kind of fade and go speckled . . . so beautiful. So, I met Sharon and Dan at the flower market one Sunday and filled my van to the brim with gorgeous vintage hydrangea heads. I set them up in buckets in my garage to dry so they kept their shape. Every day I would give the heads a quick scrunch to see if they were starting to feel dry and papery, and sure enough within a couple of weeks they were beautiful and dried and were still full heads without going all shrivelly.

Funnily enough though, so far I've only managed to make and hang one hydrangea cloud!! Which isn't to say that I won't complete the vision or that the hydrangeas don't have a place in the new Sweet Cafe. I've put them in baskets and accepted that it will be a while before I make them into clouds.

Having these hydrangeas around me constantly for months has, of course, inspired a cake design! The colours of them, the movement they give from the way they remind me of butterflies . . . I wanted to put this to use.

The design is very simplistic, and gives a vintage feel. I decided to go with a slightly cream-coloured ganache, and leave it semi-textured with raw-textured edges at the top of each tier.

Because I wanted to show off all the qualities of the hydrangeas, I thought I would use them in a couple of different ways. I would pick individual flowers from the hydrangea heads and attach them to the ganache like appliqué, in a semi-random pattern moving up the cake. This would bring out the colours and the textures beautifully and lead the viewer's eye up to the top of the cake, where I wanted to attach more of the individual flowers to florist wire so that it felt like they were blowing off the cake and giving the impression of fluttering butterflies. The sprays of 'butterfly' hydrangeas would add drama to the design—and as you know I am all about drama!

I was inspired to practise on a piece of textured paper to see how the different colours and shapes of the hydrangeas would look. I photographed it as part of my mood board, but let's just say I am currently looking for a frame to hang it in the store as a piece of art!

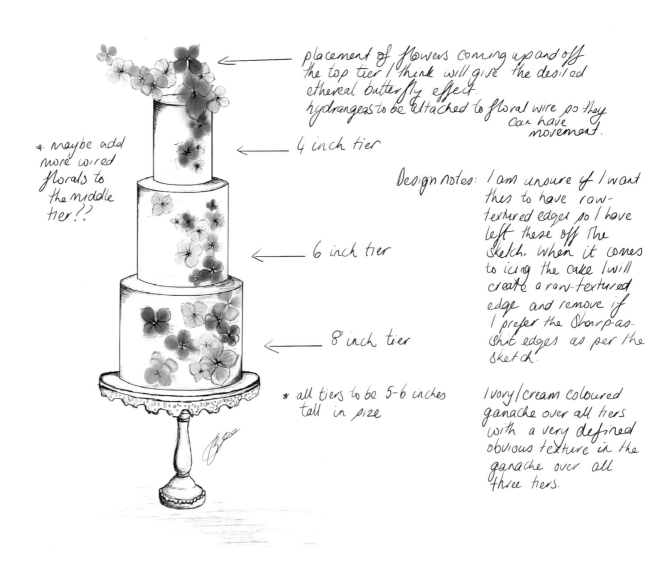

placement of flowers coming up and off the top tier I think will give the desired ethereal butterfly effect.
hydrangeas to be attached to floral wire so they can have movement.

maybe add more wired florals to the middle tier??

4 inch tier

6 inch tier

8 inch tier

all tiers to be 5-6 inches tall in size

Design notes: I am unsure if I want this to have raw-textured edges so I have left these off the sketch. When it comes to icing the cake I will create a raw-textured edge and remove if I prefer the sharp-as-chit edges as per the sketch.

Ivory/cream coloured ganache over all tiers with a very defined obvious texture in the ganache over all three tiers.

DESIGN DEBRIEF

This cake mostly developed as I imagined it. It is even very similar to the sketch. One of the most obvious changes I made was a subtle ombré in the colours used for the tiers. There's a cream-coloured ganache on the bottom, which I had intended for all three tiers—but when it came to icing the cakes, I felt that the hydrangeas would lose their interest if the whole cake remained one colour. Making the second tier subtly lighter, and the top tier almost fully white, helped with this. It changed the way the flowers looked pressed flat against the ganache.

The wired flowers coming out the top of the cake really give me the feeling of fluttering butterflies, exactly as I wanted them to. This is one of my favourite designs in the book; it has a soft, romantic feel to it, but I also love it for the textures and colour variations that nature has created in the dried hydrangeas—which have come away as the hero of the design.

JAPANESE-INSPIRED DESIGN

Back to Japan—what absolute inspiration eye-candy! Textures, history, buildings, art, flowers . . . the Japanese really are an incredible nation of inspiration. I've used aspects of our family trip to Japan in other designs, but now I wanted to really deep-dive and make use of all the inspiration pictures I took. I wanted to go FULL JAPAN.

While we were there we visited a lot of historic buildings, temples, castles, gardens and so on. I was in my element: the lines of the buildings, the use of gold throughout; even our Airbnb in Kyoto provided extensive inspiration. The traditional buildings have such wonderful architecture, including the lines and the shapes of their roofs, and how the roofs are layered so it seems like there are multiple buildings stuck together on multiple levels. I never saw the inside of most of them—but oh, the exteriors. I could stand for hours finding new intricate details to look at.

One castle had ornate gold trim around the eaves offset with a kind of light jade tile on the roof itself. I am unsure whether the roof tiles were actually jade or if that colour developed with age. However it came about, it was stunning.

A lot of the castles and temples are surrounded by huge ancient stone walls, just *so* old. You can see the damage time has caused all over them, but somehow this adds extra intricacy to the overall look and feel. Huge cracks, some with plants growing out of them, being reclaimed by nature. Painted wood that has faded into beautiful streaks and been worn by the weather to create an ombré feeling.

I was almost at a loss as to how to capture into a single design all of the feelings, experiences and wonder at what I saw in Japan. I didn't want it to be literal; I wanted it to hint at what I've described above.

I started by creating a list of the aspects of inspiration I wanted to focus the design on:

- ornate gold eaves
- the triangular shapes of the roofs
- jade colour
- broken stone.

The wallpaper in our Kyoto Airbnb had this beautiful texture with kind of a gold splatter effect over the top. I wanted to try to capture this, but I thought I would try to use the broken stone look on one tier, etching in some of the deep cracks, then using a holey sponge to dab some metallic gold over the top. This would be great starting from the bottom tier, then having some of the stone design moving up to the second tier.

I wanted to bring in the jade colour on the second tier too—large brush-strokes moving up to give a faded, weathered ombré effect. On one side I would like to script a Japanese poem in Japanese characters over pieces of gold leaf:

ONO NO KOMACHI (825–900)
Thinking about you,
I slept and saw you
In the dream.
If I had known it was a dream,
I would not have awakened.

思ひつつ 寝ればや人の 見えづらむ 夢と知りせば 覚めざらましを

Omoi tsutsu / Nu re baya hito no / Mie zu ram / Yume to shiri seba / Same zara mashi wo

On the top tier I wanted to focus on the triangles and ornate gold of the eaves of the castle we visited. Using ganache as oil paint and my cake-detailing palette knives, I would build up texture in a loose triangle style focused on one corner of the top tier. When the ganache was dry I would then highlight some of the texture with metallic gold.

Thinking about this design and its inspirations took me right back to Kyoto and I literally couldn't wait to start on the actual cake. I truly love having so much content that I have collected and experienced. Being able to use it to create designs means that I forever get to go back to those times and memories and relive them.

Square tiers
- top tier 4 inch
- middle tier 6 inch
- bottom tier 8 inch
* all tiers approx. 5 inches tall

Design details.
- gold foil in patches over top two tiers focusing along the stone design coming up onto the second tier.

- Japanese poem to be written in Japanese characters. Poem name: Ono no Komachi (825-900)

meaning: Thinking about you, I slept and saw you In the dream. If I had known it was a dream, I would not have awakened

- Stone look with lots of texture, cracks and fissures. Stone look coming up onto second tier, teal painted detail with brown kinda like wood detail from mood board.

- top tier with abstract guilded roof top of Japanese building.

DESIGN DEBRIEF

This cake is proof of how realism can lead design. There was so much I wanted to fit onto the cake, which of course was impossible but I always try nonetheless. I never want to be too exacting with a design; I'm always trying to use inspiration to create rather than copy.

In this case I definitely got caught up in the specific features I wanted to highlight. The cracked stone, the teal paint, the classic Japanese castle roof. So I put them ALL on the cake and I loved how they came out—there is no doubt what the inspiration is for this cake. My one regret is that I couldn't fit the poem into the design. On an already crowded, literal design I just couldn't add another element.

That said, while I was standing back and pondering the conundrum of not being able to add the poem, I still had this feeling that the design was missing something. In classic Bets style I started looking around me and wandering about aimlessly. I have to assume that when I do this my eyes are taking in everything and mentally adding it to the cake design to see if what I am seeing is the missing piece to the design puzzle. Suddenly, I saw my newly purchased little dried pink larkspur flowers. They seemed so very Japanese and reminded me of Japanese blossoms. I did that little squeal thing and started muttering to myself while hustling back to the cake to add the final piece of the puzzle.

MASCULINE ABSTRACT DESIGN

LET'S GET EDGY. (In more ways than one . . .)

I think that cake designs typically lend themselves to being classified as feminine. But it is important to remember that CAKE IS ART and the design can be ANYTHING. Feminine or masculine, soft and romantic, or edgy and abstract.

I have been so inspired by lines, '70s colour schemes and patterns, colour blocking, mustards, oranges, navy blues . . . The inspiration for this design actually came from loads of different places. In preparation for this book, and also 'just because', I have been carrying my camera with me in case something inspires my creativity. Also because I love flowers and nature. Who doesn't want a computer full of cool, pretty photos labelled 'inspo'?

For this design journey I want to talk through the mood board and what aspects I chose to highlight in the final design.

The colour scheme was inspired by the artwork of New Zealand artist Frances Hodgkins (1869–1947). My publisher Jenny actually recommended that I go and check out an exhibition of her works at the Auckland Art Gallery—which was just so amazing. I dragged Charlotte with me, although dragged isn't really the right word because art is her thing so she was happy to be seen in public with me that day. Frances' art was so varied. There were beautiful textured works, pencil drawings, landscapes, still-lifes, and some more abstract interpretive pieces. The painting titled *Mimosa* (see top left) inspired a colour scheme and a soft abstract layering that I knew I could depict on cake. I also loved the addition of a few seemingly random lines over the watercolour style.

Once I had chosen this image from my inspo folder I moved on to another picture of a cool vase that was on display at the art gallery (see top right). It was within the Frances Hodgkins exhibition, but I can't be sure if it was created by Frances and I don't want to be misquoted as saying it was her work. What I love about this picture in its entirety is the quirky shape of the vase, the plywood shelf it is sitting on with the lines showing, the shape of the shelf and the vibrant colours of the vase against the dark background of the wall.

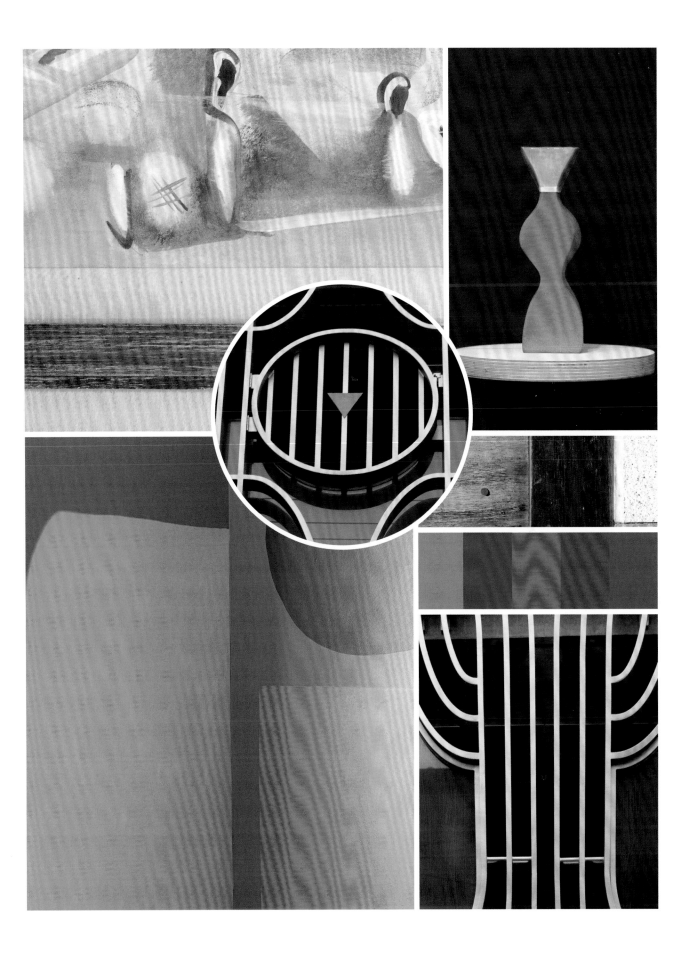

In the circle below the vase and at bottom right are pictures of a building I saw in Kyoto, Japan. I remember being focused the whole trip on capturing content for my 'inspo' album, even when we were walking to our accommodation. Classic tourists Harley, Charlotte and I, dragging our suitcases along cobbled footpaths and making a hell of a racket. When I saw this building I instantly knew I had to photograph the Art Deco style design with all the lines. I distinctly recall Harley getting pissy at me—we had just got off a train, then out of an Uber and he just wanted to get to our accommodation. Let's just say I won, and got my inspo picture regardless of pissy husband.

I didn't have a specific design in mind for this image, but it fitted in perfectly with the abstract design I wanted for this cake. I wanted to incorporate lines overlaying the colours inspired by Frances' work.

Wow, this is a real breakdown of image descriptions . . . bear with me and enjoy the journey.

The last image that really got the juices flowing was a picture I took while I was in Christchurch for a workshop led by Hannah Jensen (see the bird cake on page 44). The workshop was held at the home of designer and blogger Julia Atkinson-Dunn, which is the most creative space inside and outside. (Serious garden envy, and OMG her cat Tonks, who I wanted to catnap and take home with me!) As ever I could see cake designs in everything, so asked Julia if I could wander around her house and garden with my camera. She of course obliged, and you will see a few pictures taken in her home that I am using throughout the book as inspiration. This one in particular (see bottom left of mood board) is a photo of a wall in Julia's front room. I love it for the shapes, vibrant '70s-style colours and colour blocking.

Together, all these pictures inspired the abstract, more masculine cake you will see in the coming pages.

As well as having the lines overlaid on the glorious, rich colours of the cake, I also wanted to bring more abstract lines into the design by using a mixture of square and round tiers. Also, I would not restrain the lines and shapes to the body of the tier—I wanted there to be some abstract shapes extending at angles above the tier.

It's really important to remember to always have your eyes open. Really *look* at your surroundings, and if you see something—a colour, a texture, a shape, a flower, design, art, literally anything—snap a quick picture. Keep an 'inspo' album to flick through and link ideas from.

You might not be ready to get creative right now, or even have a project to work on—but take it from me: my collecting of cool shit has really helped to inspire the designs you see here in this book, and likely for many cakes yet to be designed in the future.

Design notes:
- black disks of chocolate placed randomly against and sticking out in places. This will add to the abstract nature of the design.

- hand-painted lines in various places over all tiers in black.

6 inch square 8 inches tall with raw-textured edges.

4x6 inch rectangle tier lying down

6 inch round 4 inch tall

10 inch square 5 inch tall

* not sure about the colour layout? may change it to be dark to light bottom to top?

DESIGN DEBRIEF

This started out as a clutter of ideas and inspirations, with the idea of 'masculine abstract' as the general direction. I used little pieces of those inspirations and visuals from the mood board to sketch together a more cohesive design concept, relying heavily on the structures of the cake and the bold colours to create the abstract masculinity I was going for. The end design differs in the arrangement of the colours of the tiers. I decided that the darkest, most dominant colour would be best on the bottom tier. Then, as I was icing the teal tier I chose to do a reverse raw-textured edge as I knew I wanted this tier to be offset and hang over the front edge of the bottom tier.

My original thoughts about design ideas didn't include the black discs, but as I was sketching I felt that the design could benefit from these. Bringing the ganache from each tier up on to the next tier was done on a whim, and I LOVE IT! It makes the tiers seem more inclusive while still remaining strong and abstract.

The lines and drawings were always meant to be freestyled and hand-painted. The idea was there to do an abstract face, which is shown in the sketch, but having the freedom to just put lines wherever I wanted was great.

POLISH KIWI WEDDING

This cake was booked in almost a year ahead—and I truly left it until the last couple of weeks before designing it. The same really goes for most of what I do. Can't force the design and can't force the creativity.

Mostly I have learned to trust myself on this, but it is harder and more stressful when there are customers involved. Lucky for me I have some *incredible* customers who say those words: 'We are happy to give you freedom with the design'. Don't mind if I do, thanks!

Martyna is one of our long-standing regulars at Magnolia Kitchen, and she asked me to make her wedding cake at a book-signing for my first book. Y'all know how long ago *that* happened. The only real must-haves for the cake were: vegan, made by me, and of course the wedding date, a Saturday in January 2020.

While I'd thought about the details Martyna gave me about herself, her fiancé Daniel and their wedding, it wasn't until she sent through a picture of the traditional Polish floral headband she was going to wear that the creativity I had been waiting for began to spark. I now knew exactly how I wanted to represent the couple in the design and create something I knew they would both love.

The main details I wanted to focus on were the gold design on their wedding invite and the traditional Polish flowers. I got to work researching Polish weddings and some of the traditions, as it was obvious to me that Martyna had specifically wanted to represent her home in her wedding. This is where the inspiration really hit. Online, I found all these beautiful pictures of Polish wedding dresses . . . just *so* stunning . . . all in white with brightly painted and embroidered floral designs. A lot of the brides wore flower crowns in bright, wild colours similar to the one Martyna had shown me.

Digging around some more, I found a picture of a Polish folk-art floral design, and this is what I used as the inspiration for the final design. Here's what I sent to Martyna and Daniel for final approval:

- *3 tiers, 9, 7 and 5 inches, round cakes*
- *Approx. 60 dessert serves / 120 coffee serves*

Whitened ganache covering on all cakes, with hand-painted Polish floral wreath design over all three tiers (as seen on wedding dresses). Accented with gold-dipped gypsophila and fresh florals around the painting to give a 3D effect, and additional gold dots in among the painted florals.

All the cakes were vegan, and there were some awesome flavours:
1. Chocolate cherry cake layered with cherry amaretto compote and vegan dark chocolate ganache
2. Strawberry vanilla bean cake layered with strawberry compote and vegan white chocolate ganache
3. Passionfruit cake layered with vegan white chocolate ganache

Hopefully you can picture in your imagination and see from the mood board what I planned. Now turn the page to reveal the sketch and then finally the finished creation.

Design notes:

- VEGAN ivory white chocolate ganache over all three tiers with raw-textured edges.

- hand-painted flowers in colour block style, bright vibrant colours

- flowers to form an oval shape spanning over all three tiers

- small amount of small fresh flowers placed amongst the painted flowers.

- small dots of gold paint in amongst the painted and fresh flowers.

- whole design inspired by Polish folk florals.

Sizes: top tier 5 inch round
middle tier 7 inch round
bottom tier 9 inch round.

All tiers approx. 5-6 inches tall

DESIGN DEBRIEF

For this cake there isn't much to debrief—it really went very much in the direction I had intended for it. The only thing that didn't work as I had imagined in my design description was the gold-dipped gypsophila. It just didn't work and so I abandoned it, and I must say the finished cake is better for that decision.

BAS RELIEF DESIGN

The starting point for this cake was a couple of words: 'white' and 'tall'. I was going to say 'simplistic', but that's not something I would usually associate with a design by me. Even if I intend it to be simplistic, I can't help going off on design tangents. Or from stepping back and thinking 'yes, yes, this needs a little extra something something ...' MORE IS MORE.

So, the focus for this design became bas relief, floral and slightly Grecian. Bas relief is one of those designs that is both beautiful from afar and interesting up close, as you discover the detail in the moulding. Of course, being me I just had to take the concept of bas relief and incorporate flowers into my design.

I have made many bas relief cakes and cookies over the years, and it is a design I love creating. I was originally inspired by one of my favourite cake decorators, Maggie Austin, who is the epitome of talent. Her designs are *so* romantic and show another side to finding inspiration in textures and buildings. I will also say that her sugar floral work is second to none; I have done a few of her online courses and she is a wonderful teacher!

It has been a long time since I created sugar flowers, as I now prefer to use fresh or dried flowers in my designs, but I learned a lot from Maggie and was happy to put it to good use.

I decided that I wanted to keep this a very classy design with some fresh white flowers and maybe a touch of greenery to liven it up. I wanted to focus the bas relief around the tops of the tiers, almost framing them but with a few stray moulds coming down onto each tier below.

The florals I would cluster from the top tier like a waterfall coming down ... maybe some nice white orchids. The ganache and the bas relief would be white on white.

As the ideas flowed, I resisted the need to add metallic ... did it need it? I didn't know, but I do love a beautiful champagne gold leaf on white. Turn over the page to see what I eventually decided. Four tiers in all its glory: another showstopper.

Thanks to Abby (moonchild) Phimsena from the Magnolia Kitchen team for providing the images of the bas relief walls in the mood board opposite. Those photos were taken on her travels in Europe.

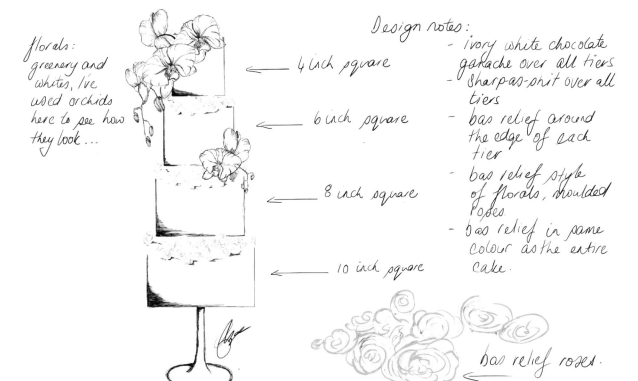

florals:
greenery and
whites, I've
used orchids
here to see how
they look ...

4 inch square

6 inch square

8 inch square

10 inch square

Design notes:
- ivory white chocolate
  ganache over all tiers
- sharp-as-shit over all
  tiers
- bas relief around
  the edge of each
  tier
- bas relief style
  of florals, moulded
  roses.
- bas relief in same
  colour as the entire
  cake.

bas relief roses.

DESIGN DEBRIEF

Let's just say that for me this cake was a complete mind-fuck and that is okay! In my defence, I did say that simplistic wasn't usually associated with my designs, and I also said MORE IS MORE! Haha—I should have known, right?!

The only parts I think I managed to stay true to were the 'bas relief' and 'white on white'. Even the sketch shows a square cake, whereas I have created a round cake (that was actually a mistake; in my head it was always supposed to be round!). I went completely off-script and let the moulding lead me. I had planned to confine the bas relief to the top of each tier, and that looked good on the sketch—but it just didn't feel right as I started to actually create it. And about two-thirds of the way into the moulding I knew I was going to add the champagne gold leaf.

Now, fresh white flowers and greenery? NOPE! I had some white orchids but they just seemed too understated. I looked over at my bucket of flowers and spotted the bright-red anthuriums, and knew that these would be the perfect addition—a statement piece. Then I looked over again and saw some willow branches. It's funny how often I convince myself that a design is complete, then add one last aspect to it and wonder how the cake had ever looked finished without it! The willow brought even more height to the design, along with more direction.

WELSH KIWI WEDDING

This cake was designed for Lewis and Nancy, who got married at Batch Winery on Waiheke Island in Auckland just a few days before New Zealand went into lockdown because of Covid-19.

Who are Lewis and Nancy to me? Well, that is a story in itself and why the creative journey for this cake was so important. Lewis came into my life around the time we were gearing up to release my first book. I had seen the videography and editing work he had done for another friend's business, and it reminded me that I had this grand scheme to create some online courses and needed a film and editing crew to help me do it. I slid into the Film Lab's DMs on Instagram and we jacked up a meeting ... from there it was a whirlwind friendship that soon included his right-hand crew-man and bestie Craig, and of course his darling then-girlfriend Nancy.

I remember Lewis telling me he was going to propose to Nancy while on holiday introducing her to his family in Wales. It was so fucken romantic ... Of course Nancy said yes and the planning ensued! I didn't expect to be doing the cake honours as Lewis's mum is herself a caker/baker back in Wales, and that was totally fine by me—I was just excited to attend my friends' wedding. But then it transpired that my services would indeed be required ...

I took a very relaxed approach, and actually didn't design the cake until a couple of days before the wedding haha. I sent a few half-assed emails asking them some key details about colour schemes and servings required, but really I knew this would be a very on-the-fly design as it was so personal and I knew the people I was designing for very well. Luckily they left me to it and mostly trusted me, although I think my lax approach was probably an added stress for Nancy at the time (sorry about that, Nancy xx). To be fair, there was a lot going on at the time with the pandemic.

Nancy had expressed a liking for a specific cake I had posted on Instagram, so that triggered some of the design. I knew the guys would be in navy and the girls in mustard. As soon as I heard the colour scheme I knew where I wanted to go with the design. It went something like this (in the absence of actually getting approval from the customer):

Ivory white ganache over all three tiers with raw-textured edge finish, overlaid with navy-coloured ganache leaving a diagonal textured window spanning over three tiers that is free of navy and allows the ivory to show through. This diagonal window will be hand-painted with mustard-coloured florals. Addition of fresh or dried florals maybe?

Once I had this rough idea in my head, I started thinking about flowers as inspiration for the painting bit. I immediately knew I wanted to paint some kowhai purely because of their yellow colour—but that got me thinking . . . the kowhai is a native New Zealand flower and Nancy is a Kiwi, so these could represent her. Then I went on a mission to find a yellow flower that was native to Wales. The obvious choice would have been a daffodil, but that didn't really have the vibe I was going for. After some googling and research I found the Welsh poppy—and it couldn't have been more perfect: mustard yellow in colour and kind of floaty. I decided I wanted to have the poppies at the bottom coming up and then the kowhai dangling down. I also had some dried yellow bobble things that I wanted to incorporate because the colour matched so perfectly. I wasn't at all sure how I was going to use them so just decided to figure it out on the day—I kind of like to get started, then stand back and assess what the design needs to complete it.

As we got closer to the date, I really felt for the couple as Lewis—being Welsh—had a lot of guests intending to travel to New Zealand for the wedding and that was all up in the air. To be honest, it was heartbreaking to watch my friends see their beautiful wedding, which was intended to be a celebration with a huge number of friends and family, be reduced significantly in numbers—although it was still a celebration regardless!

But it all worked—the big day went ahead with reduced capacity, there were video speeches and LOADS of food and cake for those of us able to attend. It was a beautiful day and the bride and groom said their I do's in the autumn sun over on Waiheke. It was so incredible to see the wedding go ahead and the beauty shine through despite the stressful lead-up. And what a story they have to tell now too!

As an add-on to this journey of inspiration, can I just say a *huge* congratulations to Lewis and Nancy—their wedding overcame a number of curve-balls. While it wasn't the wedding they'd originally planned, at least they got hitched and one thing we can all be thankful for (alongside good health) of course is a spectacular cake by me.

extra height to be created
using wafer paper torn
roughly &
covered with ganache
to hold it in place

Design details:
 - textured navy ganache
  "window" down entire cake

5 inch tier

- hand-painting to be focused
  down the white "window"
  Kowhai flowers to start at the top
  coming down, Welsh poppies
  coming up from the bottom
  meeting up with the kowhai

7 inch tier

9 inch tier

?? add these fun
pom pom flowers to
the top tier behind the dramatic
edge to create even more drama!

DESIGN DEBRIEF

For this design, it all transpired mostly as I imagined it would. There were just two things that developed as I was sketching the design. One was the height on the left side that I decided to create leading up from the top tier. I am always looking for more height, more drama.

I created this added height using torn wafer paper that I attached with ganache. I then iced over it with more of the navy blue ganache to ensure that the structure would stay put. The other thing I added—or, at least, at the point when I made the sketch I knew I wanted to add—was the bunch of dried yellow pom pom things. All that was left of course was for me to stand back and assess where they were going to look best. As I suggested in my drawing, they went inside the raised left side of the top tier and added the perfect amount of drama.

WEDGWOOD LACE DESIGN

First let's chat about Wedgwood—what is it? I feel it's important to discuss this first as I want you to be visualising it in your head, like you can almost be imaginarily designing along with me.

Wedgwood according to Wikipedia:

> Wedgwood, first incorporated in 1895 as Josiah Wedgwood and Sons Ltd, is a fine china, porcelain, and luxury accessories manufacturer that was founded on 1 May 1759 by the English potter and entrepreneur Josiah Wedgwood.

That's great info, Wikipedia, but it doesn't help with the visual. One moment please. Here is a bit more descriptive stuff via old mate Wikipedia:

> Wedgwood's best known product is Jasperware, created to look like ancient Roman cameo glass, itself imitating cameo gems. The most popular jasperware colour has always been 'Wedgwood blue'...
> The main Wedgwood motifs in jasperware, and the other dry-bodied stonewares, were decorative designs that were highly influenced by the ancient cultures being studied and rediscovered at that time, especially as Great Britain was expanding its empire. Many motifs were taken from ancient mythologies: Roman, Greek and Egyptian.

Okay. Now—in my words, I'll explain what inspired me about these pieces and how I planned to turn this idea into a design.

The porcelain is like a matte light blue colour, almost dusky. Then it has these beautiful striking white designs in a bas relief style so it is raised off the porcelain. Often the white is some Grecian scene, or florals around the edge of the piece.

Have a look at the mood board—you can see a couple of Wedgwood pieces I have photographed, along with other images I used for my design inspiration. The idea was to combine the inspo from the Wedgwood jasperware with white lacy florals. I decided to use piped white royal icing rather than a bas relief style, to make the design more delicate. I wanted the design to be quite feminine and almost vintage-looking, by hand-piping the white lace onto the cakes which are finished in a 'Wedgwood blue'.

One of my favourite royal icing cookie artists is SweetAmbs. Amber creates these beautiful, romantic works of art with cookies and royal icing (check her out on Insta, @sweetambs). One of my all-time favourites is a lace overlay. She pipes royal icing onto a cookie that has already been iced in a contrasting colour; then, using a paint brush, she drags the icing down to form a textured-lace-looking petal with the contrasting colour showing through. This can be layered up to form additional petals. This is a great technique for my lace florals.

For the placement of the lace, I wanted to focus the design down the centre of all three tiers of cake, in a strip approx. 10 cm (4 in) wide. The ganache would have a sharp-as-shit edge. I had been doing a lot of designs recently that have the raw-textured edge, which I LOVE. However, I felt that this design called for a nice clean sharp edge at the top of each tier.

This design would also work well with other contrasting colours . . . and the placement for the lace could be moved to a more diagonal look, or even clusters on each tier. As always, the final look develops from standing back to view the cake and deciding where more is needed.

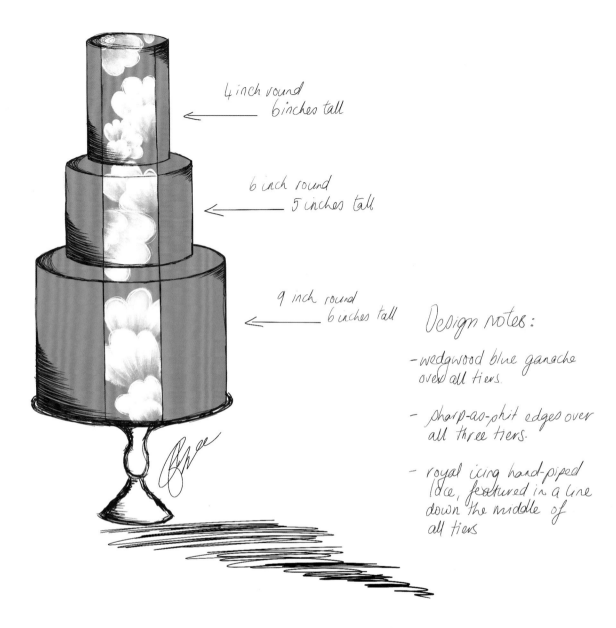

4 inch round
6 inches tall

6 inch round
5 inches tall

9 inch round
6 inches tall

Design notes:

- wedgwood blue ganache over all tiers.

- sharp-as-shit edges over all three tiers.

- royal icing hand-piped lace, featured in a line down the middle of all tiers

DESIGN DEBRIEF

The intention was there, and I think the finished design was everything I hoped it would be and more, regardless of how it differs from my concept description and sketch. I do still like the idea of containing the design to a single wide stripe down the front of the cake, but I also love the flow and spread of what I ended up creating. I sat down to start on the lace, and I guess I ended up in a sort of trance because it wasn't until I re-read the design description and looked at my sketch that I realised the cake looked nothing like I had intended. Okay, not *nothing*, but it wasn't at all constricted like I had intended and was definitely more wild. And just as wonderful.

STEP-BY-STEP
INSTRUCTIONALS

—

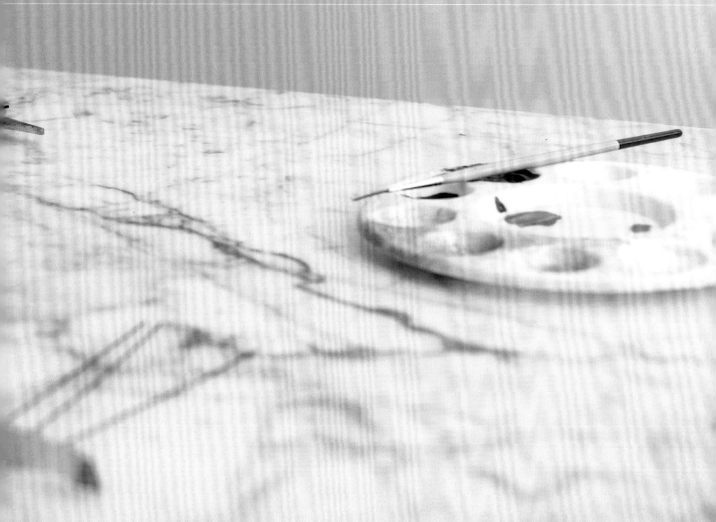

CENTRAL SUPPORT

TOOLS

3 pre-prepared cakes, each iced on a cake card with a centre hole of 12 mm diameter (THIS IS IMPERATIVE) and with a larger acrylic disc or cake card underneath

wooden dowel, 12 mm diameter

non-toxic pencil

mini saw

4 mm masonite cake board, larger than your bottom tier

1 screw—this needs to be a skinny screw approx. 20 mm long (you don't want to split your dowel)

screwdriver

masking tape

pieces of baking paper, smaller than each of the tiers

extra cake cards or acrylic discs, smaller than each of the tiers

small cake tin (smaller than the middle tier)

metal smoothie straws

jug of boiling-hot water

compostable smoothie straws

scissors

small measuring cup

Let's start with the WHY. Why would you need to go to so much trouble to put a pole up the wazoo of your tiered cake?

Well, my friend, if you are asking that then you have never seen a tiered cake fail!! I would have experienced many, many cake fails had I not had a pole up the centre of the tiers. Let's call it a 'fail-safe', a 'cover your ass' or just 'security'.

Now, you know you want to hear my 'cake fail/centre pole saved my ass' story, right? Picture this. It's the middle of wedding season and I have overbooked myself with two wedding cakes on one day (classic Bets . . . *facepalm*). Of course, these two cakes also require delivery to opposite ends of Auckland. Now, both cakes have been tiered with this technique here and both are made with ganache ('cause you know 'it's all fucken ganache'), so I've done everything right. I've planned my route and accounted for the ridiculous traffic I might encounter, I've placed non-slip mats under my cakes as I put them in the boxes, I've put non-slip mats on the seat of the van. I'VE PREPARED *EVERYTHING*.

Anyway, I then go and deliver the first wedding cake . . . all is going well and I'm heading to my final destination in central Auckland from up north. The GPS says I'll be there in an hour and I am even ahead of schedule WOOHOO. (Y'all know that is unheard of for me.) So I'm cruising along the windy roads between Warkworth and Silverdale and I come around a blind corner to find a standstill queue of traffic. I swear my life flashes before my eyes as my brain says 'slam on your brakes and that cake is FUCKED, or don't slam on your brakes and the cake will STILL be fucked but you will also now be dead'. I go for the self-preservation option and slam on my brakes.

I manage to stop inches from the car in front of me in a squeal of tyres. As I realise that I am still alive, I look over my right shoulder to check the cake—which has shot forward in its box and is now hanging from the crossbar between the front and back seats, with the bar embedded in its top tier. I am yelling and screaming at myself as I reach over and push the cake back into place on the seat.

It now dawns on me that I HADN'T PUT THE SEATBELT ON THE CAKE! A fairly easy way to learn that seatbelts save lives! Turns out they also save cakes. I'm still about 40 mins drive from the venue so I have plenty of time to go through the stages of grief. First I'm relieved I'm alive—for a split second—and then I'm crying 'cause *fuck my life, LOOK at that cake* . . . I seriously resembled Homer Simpson yelling with his mouth wide open. Then I call my husband and yell and rage at how *fucked* I am, my business is *over*, I might as well close the doors *right now* and give up. My reputation is ruined, I might as well have just not braked . . . I'M DONE!! (I know I know, soooo dramatic!)

The next stage is to realise I am, after all, a master caker and no one knows how to fix my own fuck-ups like me! I remind myself that I have all I need with me to fix the cake. I have time to repair it, and I have spare ganache, palette knives, scrapers—literally a cake-fixing kit. I do all my deliveries with it 'cause apparently I have been preparing for this cake fail all my caking life.

I fire off quick calls to the venue and the florist to let them know I need to do a 'minor' repair job onsite. Thankfully my girl Tash from Zimzee Flowers is the florist for the day, and she makes sure to leave me a massive selection of florals just in case I have to resort to a cover-up job.

I turn up. I cut back the damage and do the most epic plastering job you've seen in your life—the cake now looks as it originally did post-disaster BEFORE FLORALS. I even decide to show the whole awful situation on Instagram. I figure it's important to know that even people you think are invincible have epic fails too. But I've learned a lot about failure along the way, and I know that it's less about the failure itself and more about how you deal with it. I wanted to look back on this experience and be proud of how I dealt with it. (The groom stopped by after I'd made my repairs and was adding the florals, so I candidly told him what had happened, in the interests of full disclosure. He was so proud of the fix-up job I'd done and agreed that you would never know!)

I learned a lot about myself that day. I learned that authenticity is key even when it has the potential to discredit your 'perfect' image. I learned that I am good at facing adversity and pressure, that I wanted to live at the cost of my art (haha)—and that the cake would have been splattered in three separate tiers against the windscreen of my van had it not been for THE CENTRE POLE. This technique was the *single* reason that this cake fail was reparable. The force of me slamming on my brakes propelled the cake AS A WHOLE UNIT forward, as opposed to separating the three tiers and having them all fly forward.

Learn from me and put a pole up the wazoo . . . that is WHY.

1. Gather all your tools.

2. Prepare to cut your dowel. Measure the height of the bottom and middle tiers. Mark the bottom-tier height on the dowel, then mark the middle-tier height starting from that first mark. When you get to the top tier, only measure two-thirds of its height as you don't want the dowel to come right to the top of cake. Mark this two-thirds height on the dowel above the middle-tier mark. The final mark is where you will cut.

3. Brace your dowel on the edge of your bench and use your saw to cut the dowel at the full marked length. Make your cut at a 45-degree angle, as this makes the dowel sharp and will help when guiding the cake onto it. Wash down your dowel with hot soapy water to make sure there is no debris on it, then dry it.

4. Most masonite cake boards have a hole in the centre. If your board doesn't have a small centre hole already, then just measure and mark the *exact* centre of the board; this is where you will put your screw. Turn the board over and pre-screw the screw into the board until approx. 2 mm protrudes out the other side.

5. Centre the flat end of your dowel against the screw, pushing it slightly so that the screw holds the dowel in place. Now for the balancing act ... I enlist my gut to hold the board on its end on the bench while I hold the dowel straight against the screw on one side and then use the screwdriver to work the screw into the dowel. When the head of the screw is flush with the board, tape some masking tape over the screw head. This will ensure that you'll be able to move the finished cake across a bench without scratching the surface.

6. This is what your finished centre-dowel board will look like—with the dowel straight up and down. Set aside and move on to cake prep.

7. Place a piece of baking paper on top of your bottom tier, then place an acrylic disk or a spare cake card on top. This will protect your cake for the next step.

8. THIS IS DEATH-DEFYING, but don't worry, it will be fine—just remember to move fast. First, place a small cake tin upside down on your bench; you will be using this to rest your cake on in a moment. Lifting the cake up, place one hand below the cake and one flat on the top, count to three, take a deep breath and flip it over.

9. Once you have your cake balanced upside down, set it down on the upside-down cake tin.

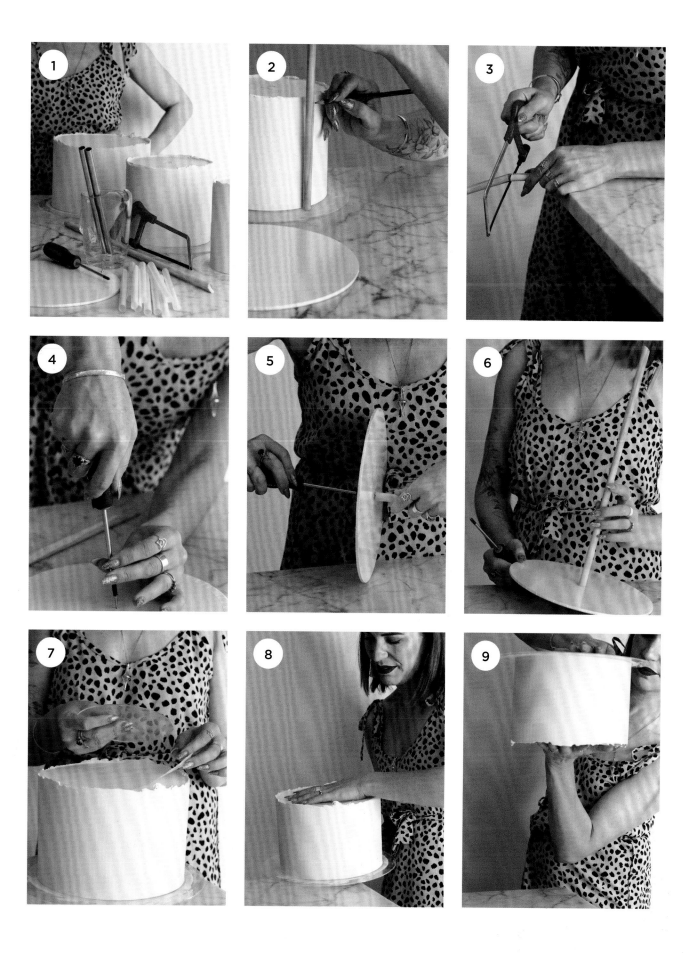

10. Remove the larger disc or cake card that you iced your cake onto, leaving the smaller cake card with the hole in the centre exposed.

11. Sit your metal smoothie straws in boiling water to heat up for a few minutes.

12. Position a heated smoothie straw in the centre of the cake board and push it straight into the cake. Make sure you keep the straw straight up and down, as this is the path the centre dowel will later follow. Continue pushing down until you reach the bottom of the cake.

13. Before you remove the metal straw, give it a few twists and move it up and down to ensure that you have made the hole straight and right to the bottom. Once you are happy with it, remove the straw and return it to the hot water to soak.

14. Now reverse step 8. Lifting the cake up, place one hand below the cake and one flat on the top, count to three, take a deep breath and flip over.

15. Remove the small acrylic disc or cake card and baking paper. You will now see that there is a straw-sized hole in the top of the cake.

16. With both hands under the cake, lift it up and over the centre-dowel board. I crouch down so that I can see the hole in the bottom to guide it onto the dowel. As you guide it, ensure that you keep the cake as level as possible—this will help the dowel stay central.

17. When you have lowered the cake to approx. 10 cm (4 in) above the masonite board, position your fingers at the very edge underneath each side of the cake, count to three, and then fast as lightning let go of the cake. I know this sounds mad, but if you have iced your cake using my recipes and instructions your cake will be fine—the ganache has a nice solid structure and can handle what seems like a violent drop onto the base. (If you lower your cake right to the board and then try to remove your hands from underneath, you will compromise the perfect edges around the base of your cake.)

18. Add your internal supports; I use compostable smoothie straws. They are eco-conscious, sturdy and load-bearing, easy to cut and easy to insert. I am working with a 23 cm (9 in) cake on the base, so I am adding six straws, evenly spaced.

19. Be careful to not place your straws outside where the next tier will sit—you don't want them to be visible. Push them right down to the bottom of the cake layer.

20. Using your pencil, mark each straw at the level of the top of the cake.

21. Pull the straws out halfway to expose the pencil mark, then cut each straw at the mark. Try to cut as straight as possible, to make things as level as possible for the next tier to sit on.

22. Push the straws back into the cake so that they are flush with the top of the cake.

23. With your second tier, repeat steps 7–16: flip the cake, place on a small tin, cut a hole in the centre with a hot smoothie straw, flip back and lower onto the dowel.

24. When you have lowered the cake to approx. 10 cm (4 in) above the bottom tier, position your fingers at the very edge underneath each side of the cake, count to three, and then as fast as lightning let go of the cake—just like you did with the bottom tier. It will glide into place and rest on top of the supports in the bottom tier.

25. Add your supports to the middle tier, following steps 18–22. I am using four straws for an 18 cm (7 in) middle tier.

26. Now for your top tier. Place some baking paper on top of your cake, then an acrylic disc or spare cake card, as before. Placing one hand on top and one on the bottom, flip your top tier over.

27. Rest your cake on a measuring cup that sits flat on your bench. Remove the larger acrylic disc or cake card that you iced your cake onto, exposing the cake card with the hole in the centre. Continue with steps 11–13, but when you push the heated smoothie straw into the cake DO NOT PUSH IT ALL THE WAY TO THE BOTTOM. You will be able to tell when you are pushing through cake (easier) and when you are pushing through the icing layer (a bit harder). So only push until you reach the second icing layer. (If you find it easier, just push down approx. two-thirds of the way through the cake.)

28. The same as you did to before, lift the cake up, place one hand below it and one flat on top, count to three, take a deep breath and flip back over. Remove the small acrylic disc or cake card and baking paper—there shouldn't be a visible hole in this tier.

29. With two hands under the cake, lift it up and over the dowel board as before to guide it on to the dowel. Again, keep the cake as level as possible to help the dowel stay central. You can use one hand against the side of the cake to help guide it down—the top tier is taller than it is wide and this makes it a wobbly little sucker. Do what you need to, but just make sure you don't have dirty fingers before touching the side of the cake!

30. Marvel at your beautiful three-tiered cake that you know is as structural as fuck! It is peace of mind on a plate (even on that precarious cake stand haha).

These instructions can be modified to allow you to put a centre pole inside a two-tier cake; just adapt the steps accordingly. The same goes if you are constructing a four-tier cake.

THE OPPOSITE OF SHARP-AS-SHIT

TOOLS

masonite board 1–2 sizes larger than your cake

Magnolia Kitchen turntable

non-slip mat

icing of your choice

Magnolia Kitchen offset spatula

3 chilled one-layer cakes, trimmed

9-inch Magnolia Kitchen sharp-as-shit scraper

AKA HOW TO CREATE RAW-TEXTURED EDGES EFFORTLESSLY

So in my last book I was all about the sharp-as-shit edges and was all teachy teach teach of the Magnolia Kitchen sharp-as-shit ways. Well, I still obsess over sharp-as-shit but the raw-textured edge is my new jam—it's close to perfection, but at the same time a little rough around the edges. A little crown of imperfection on a cake, reminding us to embrace texture in design.

You will see the raw-textured edge used throughout this book, which is why I ended up putting it in as an instructional. If you are all *waaaa* that you wanted a sharp-as-shit instructional, well my friends that is in the *other* book and it's super-extensive (including amazing detail on how to trim your cakes!). Or you can always check out my online courses if you want to see my face and have me teach you how to do it in a moving film.

I often call the main part of this process my 'ganache on ganache' technique, but it can be done with any of my buttercreams or ganaches.

1. Set up the masonite board on your turntable, with the non-slip mat between the board and the turntable to stop it slip-sliding up the wazoo.

2. Prep your icing. I'm using my delicious AF Beurre Noisette Buttercream, but you can just as easily use ganache. Make sure it is well whipped, soft and a spreadable consistency. Using your offset spatula, smear a blob of icing on the cake board.

3. Gently place your first layer of trimmed cake on the board—make sure it is bang in the centre.

4. Scoop a generous amount of icing onto the top of the cake with your spatula.

5. Spread evenly with your offset spatula until smooth and flat. You want a thickness of about 1.5 cm (⅝ in) between the layers of cake.

6. Carefully add the second layer of cake, making sure it is centred and aligned. Press it down firmly. Scoop a generous amount of icing onto the top of the cake.

7. Spread evenly with your offset spatula until smooth and flat.

8. Carefully add the third layer of cake, making sure it is centred and aligned. Press it down firmly.

9. Spread a small amount of icing around the outside layers to lock in the crumbs—this is called a crumb coating. Move your offset spatula back and forth, pushing the icing into the cake, and scrape away any excess crumb-filled icing.

10. Scoop a generous amount of icing on top of the third layer, and spread it evenly with your offset spatula.

11. Make sure it is nice and flat and smooth—this is the final top of the cake.

12. Now completely cover the sides of the cake, ensuring that your messy-as-fuck icing is at least 1.5 cm (⅝ in) thick. (This bit is why I call it ganache on ganache ... if I'm using ganache of course.)

13. Keep going until it's all nicely covered.

14. Now grab your Magnolia Kitchen sharp-as-shit scraper. Hold it at about a 60-degree angle with the edge flush against the icing but don't press too hard. Turn the turntable as you pull the scraper towards you—you want to gently scrape back the icing in quarter-turns until you have removed 50% of the excess icing. Position the scraper, do a quarter-turn, remove the icing from the scraper, wipe clean, and repeat.

15. If your raw edges aren't obvious or high enough, you can add more icing around the top with your spatula.

16. Back to scraping, and this time no stopping and starting—it's gotta be a FULL ROTATION each time from here on in. Keep doing this until the icing is completely smooth. As you scrape, the icing will push up slightly and reach above the top edge of the cake, creating the raw-textured-edge beauty.

17. Boom! And there you have your raw-textured edge.

TEXTURED GANACHE

TOOLS

pre-prepared cake

coloured ganache (1:4 ratio; see page 254), at a spreadable consistency

Magnolia Kitchen cake detailing palette knife

Magnolia Kitchen mini metal scraper

This is a technique that will always be used to some degree in my designs. It can add texture and dimension to a simple design, and can also be a great way to introduce colour.

For this design, I have added some blue ganache on the bottom tier and I want to bring that up onto the two top tiers, but not all the way. I want to add texture and colour, but I want to focus only around the bottom of the two upper tiers and leave the remaining cake white.

1. Start with your coloured ganache at a spreadable consistency. Using a palette knife, spread a small amount of ganache onto the cake where you want to add texture and/or colour. You can add as little or as much texture as you like . . . that is what is great about this technique.

2. Grabbing your mini metal scraper, hold it at approx. a 20- to 30-degree angle, with the flat sharp edge resting just forward of where you have spread the ganache.

3. Drag the mini metal scraper towards you, making sure you keep the scraper against the cake but with only a light pressure so as not to scrape too much of the texture away. Here you can see me using this technique on the top tier.

4. Repeat this process until you have the look you are going for. Work with small amounts of ganache at a time so that it keeps its spreadable consistency and you can still scrape it. If the ganache hardens on the cake you will need to apply more pressure to your mini scraper to scrape the ganache back.

INSTRUCTIONAL
OIL-PAINT GANACHE

TOOLS

pre-prepared cake

Magnolia Kitchen turntable

Magnolia Kitchen cake detailing palette knives

white chocolate ganache (1:4 ratio; see page 254), at a spreadable consistency

food colours

palette (I am using a Magnolia Kitchen acrylic disc)

Ganache, as we know, is my favourite cake-decorating medium to work with . . . in fact, at one point I was going to have T-shirts made that said 'It's all FUCKEN ganache' because the most-asked question sliding into my Instagram DMs was 'What icing is that?' And because I was asked that SO MUCH I would try to pre-empt all the questions and just yell at the beginning: 'It's ganache, ganache, ganache, IT'S ALL FUCKEN GANACHE'. Actually I think I signed a few books with that phrase too.

For me, ganache is a perfect base for a cake canvas, and it's great when using art techniques on the cake: think of it as edible oil paint. It is ideal for making designs pop and for adding textures—it can be smooth or rough—and it sets at room temp.

I have long had a love affair with creating an oil-paint style on cakes; I even have my own branded cake tools to be used for these techniques. My cake detailing palette knives have so many uses in my kitchen, but I particularly created them for this style of cake. I love the abstract feel this design style exudes—you can hint at florals and other elements without the need for perfection. Nature is imperfectly perfect, so I try not to over-think what a flower should look like and just let the ganache do its thing.

The ganache adds the elements of movement, texture and depth, but the *colours* also play a huge part in the overall effect. I like to dump small piles of base white ganache on my acrylic palette (which is just a repurposed acrylic cake disc). To approx. three piles I will assign shades for the petals, usually having a spare pile too; then a green pile, maybe two, for the leaves; brown for branches; and yellow for centres if required. When I mix the colours I try *not* to go for uniformity—some bits are mixed in, some are left dark and some are left as the base white. They get mixed more as you use them, but as you add them to the cake the different colours through each pile give it less of a 'paint by numbers' feel. I absolutely love to photograph the finished palette after the cake is complete—the mess is beautiful and I feel it is part of the art!

For the cake in this step-by-step I had an image that I'd picked up from a flower reference book of a blossom-style branch. I had a loose image in my head of how I wanted it to look on the cake but I also let the design lead me, while always having a direction in mind for the finished product.

I like to treat my designs as if I were the client or a guest viewing the cake. By this I mean always think about the journey their eyes will take while viewing the cake—you don't want it to feel disjointed and broken.

1. I am using a three-tier cake with varying heights, finished with my 'ganache on ganache' technique with raw-textured edges (see page 110).

2. Starting with piles of plain white ganache that is soft and spreadable, roughly mix with the colours you'll be using. These don't need to be fully mixed—in fact, it's better if they're not. Make sure you keep a spare white ganache pile for adjusting the shade of your colours to add dimension on the cake.

3. Don't be afraid of the first petal—just get straight into it. This is a great picture of how I like to hold my palette knife. It allows me to control the pressure as I press the ganache onto the cake. Start with a pea(ish) size dab of ganache and touch it gently against the cake.

4. Using a smearing motion, create a small semi-circle with gentle but firm pressure—you don't want to gouge into the cake, but you do want the ganache to adhere to it. You can see that there is some ganache that has extended above the palette knife—this creates the illusion of depth on the petal, almost like the top edge is folding over on itself.

5. Repeat for the next petal, overlapping the first one slightly. You can see how I've have changed the way I'm holding the knife to account for the angle and the fact that I am not working on a flat surface. I am aiming for approx. four petals per blossom, but depending on the direction I have the flower facing it might have fewer.

6. On to the fourth petal ... when you're adding more ganache, don't be afraid to scoop a light colour or even some of the base white into the mix as you add the petals. This will give the design added depth.

7. Add a small amount of yellow ganache with a little touch to the centre.

8. Here's a single completed blossom. You can see some lighter peach colour and then a deep, almost pinky-peach throughout the petals. Also notice the ruffle-y textured edges on the tips of the petals.

9. See here how I have avoided over-mixing the colour through my piles of ganache? I'll be using the darker peach one next.

10. Now for a larger blossom with a more random style. Here I've started with a large semi-circle using the darker peach ganache. I loaded a *lot* of ganache onto my palette knife in the hope that it would extend out over the edge to create a good overhang on the petal.

11. Next I've gone over the same petal with the lighter peach, being careful not to disrupt the overhang I created with the darker colour.

12. Here I am adding a leaf with green ganache, by adding it directly over the centre of the petal and then dragging the ganache diagonally downwards and away.

13. Add a yellow centre right at the edge of the leaf.

14. Build up additional petals either side of the leaf to bulk out the blossom.

15. Here I've added another leaf, slightly lower down, to finish the blossom. This is a classic example of using nature as a guide but not replicating it. I don't know about you guys, but to me it's kind of a weird-ass-looking blossom—but once you get more blossoms and buds and petals on the cake it just seems to work. I encourage you to just get it on there, then step back and take in the cake as a whole rather than looking at the individual blossoms.

16. Start adding a few sideways blooms; these can just be one or two petals.

17. Using the same technique as in step 4, work with semi-circular motions. Try some larger semi-circles and some smaller to vary the sizes of the petals.

18. Make sure you use all the varying shades of ganache—see how the top petal closest to the full blossom it has a lighter-shaded petal directly overlapping a darker one.

19. This blossom is sort of sideways . . . I started with a lighter peach and then layered darker peach petals on top.

20. I've added a small amount of yellow to the sideways blossom from step 19, to help show that it's open but just a side view. Now start adding little leaves to the bases of the blossoms. I've started with what looks like a little blossom bud, with the leaf covering half of the bud.

21. To form the leaves, just push the green gently onto the blossom and drag away sideways or down, depending on the direction you want the blossom or bud to be angled at.

22. Remember—you're not aiming for a perfect replication of a blossom tree! This is an ABSTRACT technique to hint at what the client or guest should see in the design. So don't over-think your flower placement or leaf shapes.

23. Now start moving the design up the cake as if a branch is reaching up sparsely over the tiers.

24. When creating this style, I try to have a few statement blossoms or flowers and then fill out with side views and buds.

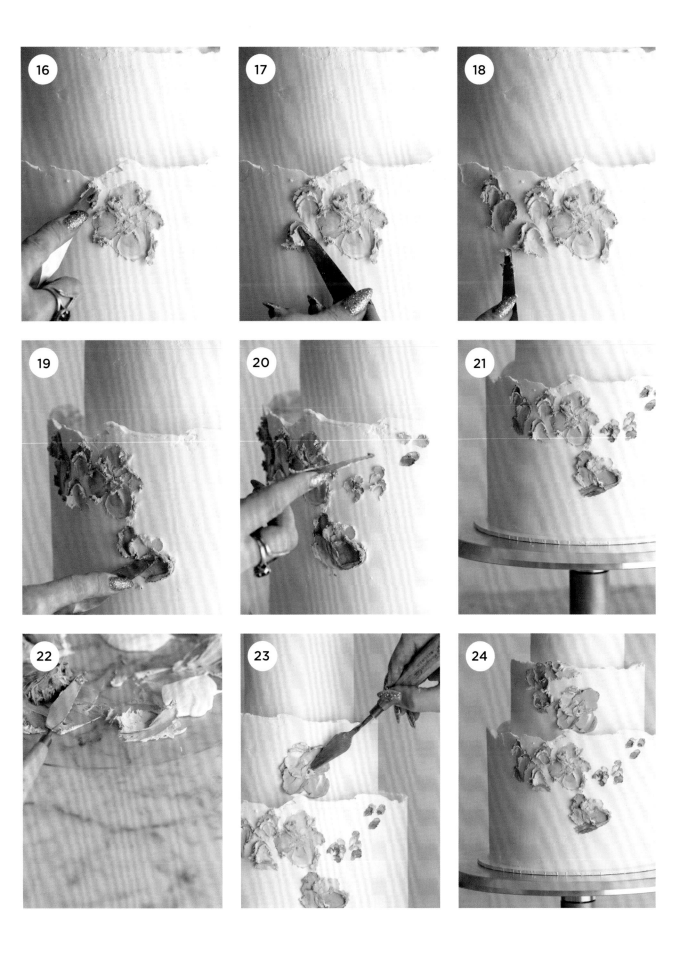

25. When you are satisfied with your blossoms and leaves, it's time to add some branches. Here I have mixed a dark brown and am starting to add it.

26. Use different parts of the palette knife to make sure you add only the right amount. Here I am using the tip of the palette knife for the thicker part of the branches, keeping it abstract.

27. Use the side edge of the palette knife to create thinner branches just by touching the ganached edge to the cake.

28. Make sure you join all the blossoms and buds with branches.

29. Stand back and look at the cake as a whole piece of art. I often like to add extra leaves or buds here and there to fill out the design or add more direction.

30. Looking closer, you can see all the wonderful different textures the ganache has created.

INSTRUCTIONAL
SPONGE-PAINTED OMBRÉ

TOOLS

pre-prepared cake

Magnolia Kitchen turntable

powdered food colour

paint palette

rose spirit

dropper

paint brushes for mixing

various sponges (I am using some face-paint application sponges, but any sponge will be fine as long as it's brand-new and doesn't come with cleaning products on it)

Magnolia Kitchen cake detailing palette knife

paper towel

I've said it before and I'll say it again: cake should be treated like a canvas. Granted it may be an edible one, but it's a canvas nonetheless.

Creating art on cake is limitless, so don't allow society to tell you what is and what isn't a cake tool or a cake-design technique. Just like working on a real canvas, the tools and techniques are transferable.

Of course this sponge technique is nothing revolutionary in the art and DIY world. I remember doing something similar to this in high-school art class, but obviously on paper and fabrics. I think it's most commonly used on wallpaper and furniture these days but hey, you know me—everything looks like a cake technique haha.

What I love about this technique is that you can really get some layers going. You can follow my example here and add multiple colours, using the sponge to blend these together slightly where they overlap. Or you can simply start with a cake in a base colour and use the sponge to overlay another colour. A dark-grey base with a sponged white colour on top would give an awesome old-stone look. You could even use multiple shades of white, grey and black to give a cool industrial finish.

I actually used this technique in my Japanese-inspired design on pages 68–73, but I changed it up slightly by using runny ganache as my 'paint' to sponge onto the cake. It turned out looking EPIC, and gave the design the extra texture and realism I was aiming for to depict the stone look.

One of the things I hope y'all are learning about me as you read this book is my love for taking traditional art and applying it to cake.

Enough of the chitchat for now: let's get down to ombré action.

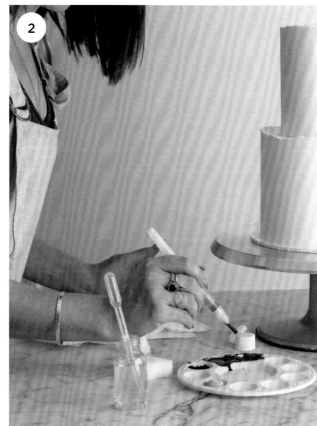

1. I am using a two-tiered cake prepared with my 'ganache on ganache' technique with raw-textured edges (see page 110).

2. Prepare your tools and get your paints ready. I used powdered food colour, and I chose to do navy blue and gold for this design.

3. Prepare your paints by adding small amounts of powdered food colour to your palette and wetting to a wet paste using drops of rose spirit (use the dropper). Rose spirit is great for painting on cakes, as it evaporates and leaves just the paint behind.

4. Using a dry sponge, dab on your first colour. I started with the navy blue at the bottom, planning to ombré up to a mustard with gold metallic. Don't worry if you make a mess on the cake board—this can be cleaned later.

5. Keep dabbing with the sponge, adding more colour around the bottom of the cake. It's like layering—you want it to be more layered and deeper in colour at the bottom.

6. Once you have a solid level of colour around the bottom of the cake, go around again a bit higher, this time keeping it a touch lighter with less layering. Repeat this as you move up the cake, adding less colour and less layering each time.

7. I like to keep going back to the bottom to layer it up more as I move up, so I get a more defined ombré with a clear fade from dark to light. Here I stopped with the first colour two-thirds of the way up the first tier.

8. When you are happy with the ombré transition of your first colour, move on to your second colour—I chose a metallic mustard.

9. Using the same dabbing method, start by layering your second colour slightly over the first colour so that they meet and overlap slightly.

10. Now move up with your second colour—you want to layer it more around the TOP of the cake, just like you did with the first colour on the bottom of the cake.

11. Layer layer layer.

12. Remember to take the colour up onto the top of the first tier before moving up to the second tier.

13. Now take the second colour up on to the second tier. Here I wanted it to extend only one-third of the way up this tier. As you get to where you are happy to stop, start to dab more lightly so as to thin out the ombré and fade it up the cake. See how I have moved back down with the mustard over the navy too, and added in a touch of metallic gold to give some pizazz.

14. Time to clean the mess made on the board! Grab your palette knife and a paper towel.

15. Fold the paper towel over the tip of the palette knife, then dampen the paper towel with rose spirit.

16. Hold the point of the palette knife flat against the board so that it is nearly touching the cake, and wipe gently. This will leave you with a sleek, clean board with tidy edges right up to the cake.

INSTRUCTIONAL
USING FRESH FLORALS

TOOLS

pre-prepared cake

Magnolia Kitchen turntable

florals

greenery

secateurs

florist tape (plastic type)

florist wire

Fun fact: my dream job is a florist, it always has been! I know that may be a shock, because I'm sure everyone assumes I'm sitting pretty doing my dream job already. Don't get me wrong, though—I love cakes, I love baking, and turns out I love running a business and being an author too. All things that I never ever planned for or imagined adding to my ever-growing list of 'talents' haha.

I've always loved nature . . . and, well, you just have to look at the name of my business to know that I love flowers—specifically the magnolia, which has long been my muse. I grew up with parents who were very garden-proud. We had a feast-producing vege garden, and the flower beds got replanted every season—which of course we kids were roped into. I don't remember loving the digging and getting dirty parts, but I do look back on it fondly and I can still remember a lot of the plant and flower names.

My granny has the most EPIC garden—she is a florist and a landscape artist. As kids, we loved playing hide and seek among her roses, although technically we weren't allowed to stray from the well-manicured grass into the flower beds. Her garage ceiling was not visible through all the hanging dried florals, and I even remember her and some friends entering a piece into the Ellerslie Flower Show. I believe it was a string quartet made from dried nikau palms and other stuff . . . Not long ago my granny was in hospital in Tokoroa, where my dad's side of the family comes from, and when I visited her I marvelled at how beautiful the magnolia trees in the hospital grounds were. She casually looked out the window and told me she'd planted those, and went on to reveal that she was the head landscaper at the hospital years ago. It's weird that all of this stuff is coming back to me as I type this . . . it makes me think how our upbringings can truly have an impact on our passions. Flowers for me are a joy, and it means a lot to me that I get to include them in my art just like my granny did.

Adding florals to cakes can seem daunting, and I get it—for a long time I would feel a sense of panic about adding that first bloom. I then learned to JUST START . . . I've found that starting with larger blooms and leafy pieces and then building from there works really well, as you can see the design begin to transform. I always try to create a natural flow, too; florals lend themselves well to a diagonal arrangement, seemingly spilling over the top of the cake.

Florals are a great way to incorporate a cake into the theme of a wedding. I always get the wedding florist to provide the flowers for the cake so that everything matches seamlessly. I am very particular about being the only person allowed to add the florals to the cake on-site—they are an extension of the design and as such should only be added by the cake decorator. I hope that this instructional gives other cakers the confidence to create beautiful floral works of art on their cakes.

1. Start with epic florals—this will depend on your design and colour scheme, of course.

2. I like to have a selection of closed blooms, large open blooms, small filler flowers and a variety of greenery.

3. Keep your stems nice and long—you will cut each one based on its placement on the cake.

4. I am decorating a three-tiered cake that has been finished with my 'ganache on ganache' technique with raw-textured edges (see page 110).

5. The tools you need are very basic but also very important, especially the florist tape—you will be wrapping each stem to ensure that no contamination from the trimmed stem will get onto the cake and be eaten (*yuck*).

6. Start by selecting the large blooms that you want to be the focus for your clusters. Leave about 8–10 cm (3¼–4 in) of stem on these larger ones, as they will protrude more from the cake—you will fill in with greenery and filler florals behind and around them.

7. I am starting with these beautiful peonies as my statement florals. I have two, so will focus on two clusters for the finished look. (For this cake there is no customer, so I get to go full-colour with no concept in mind—yippee!)

8. I prefer this plastic type of floral tape—because it is plastic it makes a good barrier and it's also a lot easier to use than the paper types. Just tear off a section and give it a gentle stretch. Then, starting at the bottom of your stem, cover the end and then begin turning the stem while keeping the tape stretched, gradually working your way up the stem. Cover about half of the length of the stem, as this is usually how much you will insert into the cake.

9. This is what your wrapped stem should look like.

10. Now hold the flower up to the cake to sort of test the best placement for it.

11. Position the stem where you will push it into the cake. If you are adding it to the top of a tier, like I am here, position it as close to where the two tiers meet as possible. If you place a large stem too close to the outside of the cake you risk it ripping through the side—so you always want to angle the stem slightly towards the centre of the cake.

12. My two clusters will start from these large florals on the bottom and middle tiers, offset from each other. First I'm going to focus on adding direction up and away from the top flower to create height and drama. I am using some willow branches for height.

13. Remember to wrap all your stems, decide where you are going to place them, and *then* push them into the cake. I've added the willow behind my statement flower and angled slightly to the left, but because the willow is so long and could be unstable due to its weight I will add additional support.

14. Cut a piece of florist wire approx. 6 cm (2½ in) long and fold it in half to make a U shape.

15. Hold the wire with the ends either side of the stem you want to support against the side of the cake. I am positioning my wire two-thirds of the way up the cake tier for maximum support. Push the wire in so that it sits fully against the stem and prevents the stem falling forwards.

16. This is what the support wire looks like when it is in place. You can do this with stems as well as greenery—it just adds support for heavier pieces or ones that aren't pointing in quite the right direction.

17. Now start thinking about filler flowers. There is a lot of exposed stem poking out of the cake, and the aim is to camouflage this with extra greenery and filler flowers.

18. ALWAYS STOP TO SMELL . . . I've picked stock for some of my smaller filler flowers, and I tell you it is one of my favourite scents. Stock smells like sweet spices and reminds me of cloves.

19. Before trimming your stems, always test where you plan to place each flower on the cake—this will give you an idea of how long the stem needs to be. AND, always tape as you go.

20. Recheck your placement before inserting the flower into the cake. I am adding this one slightly higher than the statement flower, and bridging the gap between that and the willow which I have used for height and drama.

21. Notice how from the side the exposed stems are showing. The filler greenery and florals will help to conceal this.

22. Up until now, all stems have been inserted into the top of a tier. Now I am adding some filler to the side of the cake. This is purely about direction—I want this piece to be directed downwards so that there is direction in the finished cluster. Again, the stem will be concealed with more filler florals and greenery.

23. Be careful not to overcrowd your clusters. I am choosing my fillers so that they add *dimension*. The hellebores are kind of floppy and droopy, so give the perfect fill and dimension rather than being too tight with the other florals.

24. I know I've said this before, but always test to get the right stem length before cutting and taping. For the hellebores at the the top, I kept the stems longer to add the height I wanted. At the bottom of the clusters, I shortened the hellebores to cover some exposed stems.

25. There is a lot of 'winging it' involved, and it comes down to personal preference as to when you stop adding to your clusters. I am notorious for overfilling, so have kept it 'less is more' for this step-by-step. IT IS OKAY not to use every bloom. I desperately wanted to use this purple freesia, but it just didn't vibe with the cake when I tried to add it. Don't be scared to remove something that doesn't work, either.

26. As you keep adding to your clusters, really think about the directions and dimensions. Here I am focusing all the height of the willow and the hellebores to the left side of this top tier.

27. You can really see the direction in this close-up of the top tier.

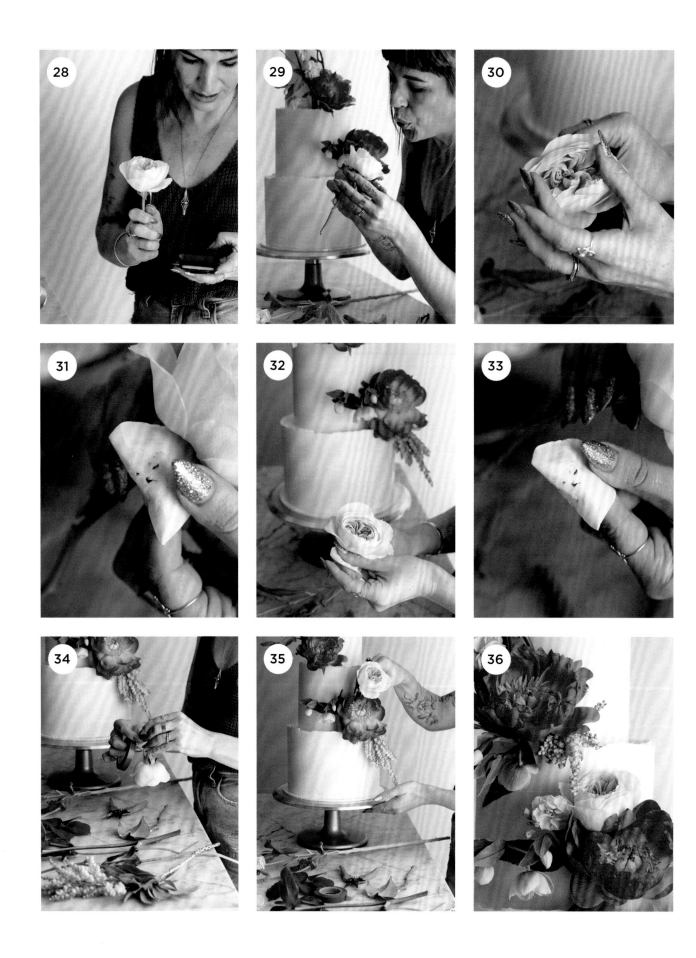

28. Roses are perfect for large statement florals or as smaller fillers. I believe this one is a David Austin, though honestly I could be making that up, but it kind of has these four partitions of petals inside. It smelt incredible, so I've clearly stopped to 'gram about it.

29. I've seen florists 'blow their blooms' when I have been on-site setting up for weddings, and I believe it's done to encourage a flower to open gently without bruising the petals. So I am doing this to try to make the rose a little more open to fill a space in my lower cluster.

30. You can also give it a wee spread with your hands, but be gentle, as the petals on roses and other flowers can bruise easily—and then they go brown and yuk.

31. Always check the outer petals, as these are often the first to be damaged in transit or from over-handling. Here's an example of a damaged petal.

32. It's important to make sure that anything added to the cake is enhancing the design. You can see that removing the damaged petal won't affect the balance of the bloom.

33. Grasp the petal between finger and thumb, and gently pull to remove it from the base cleanly rather than ripping it.

34. Did you remember to ALWAYS TAPE AS YOU GO?

35. See how I'm still focusing on direction and dimension? I'm adding this medium-size rose above and slightly left of the statement peonie of the bottom cluster, because I want to make the gap between the two clusters slightly smaller.

36. Here you can see how seamlessly the two clusters seem to be directed towards each other.

INSTRUCTIONAL
CAKE
ILLUSTRATIONS

TOOLS

prepared illustration
on paper

lightbox or window

masking tape

non-toxic pencil

craft knife

pre-prepared cake

Magnolia Kitchen
turntable

paint palette

edible paint

fine paintbrushes

Me: How on earth am I going to teach everyone how to draw freehand on a freaken cake?

Bruce: Why don't you show them how to trace images/illustrations onto the cake instead of freehand?!!

Me: Bruce, you bloody beaut, you truly are the Messiah.

Now, if you are in doubt about your freehand drawing skills but have always wanted to get artistic on a cake, then this technique is for you.

Way back when I figured out that cake was, for me, just another type of canvas I had serious doubts about my ability to draw. Okay, I knew I could draw and paint, as I've done this all my life, but there will always be self-doubt. So I would use this tracing method to reassure myself that what I had in my mind for the design was being translated correctly onto the cake.

Obviously now I am all about freehand because my confidence in my ability has grown hugely, but I'm stoked to be passing this technique on to you guys—maybe one day you too will feel more confident and start freehanding.

This tracing technique can be used for any type of painted cake, whether you want to paint flowers, cartoons or lettering, etc.

1. Prepare your image—for this cake I wanted some floral image inspiration. You can research images via old mate Google or peruse some floral illustration books. I like to pick three to five different flowers and join them into one illustration. I use the computer to join these in a single document, but you can print or copy each flower individually if you need to.

2. Once you have your illustration prepared and printed, gather the rest of your tools.

3. Here I am using a frosted window with natural light coming through it. If you're fancy as fuck and have a lightbox then use that, but if you're like me just work with what ya got. Turn the illustration over so it is flat against the window and fix it in place with tape. Then use your pencil to outline your illustration. I try not to go into too much detail doing this and just focus on the main outlines, as I can fill in the detail later once it's on the cake.

4. If you want your illustration to span over multiple tiers, you will need to cut your paper down so that you can do each tier separately. I am having my illustration span over the bottom two tiers of a three-tier cake. Hold the illustration pencil-side against the cake and mark the paper at the top of the lower tier.

5. Lay your illustration out flat and cut where you have marked the top of your tier; you will now have two illustrations. If your illustrations don't require splitting, then skip this step.

6. Position your illustrations with the pencil side against the cake and use masking tape to secure them flat and against the cake. If you prefer you can secure the paper with pins, but this can leave little holes in the cake.

7. Step back from your cake and check that you are happy with the placement of your illustrations.

8. Make sure your pencil is sharpened before starting this step. Now carefully trace over the illustration, pressing lightly so that the pencil on the reverse side transfers onto the cake. You don't want to press so hard that the illustration is scored deeply into the cake—just a light indent and the pencil lines should be visible on the cake.

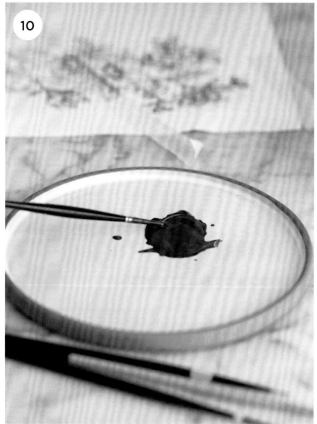

9. When you have traced over the whole illustration, gently remove the paper and masking tape to reveal the transferred outline on the cake.

10. Prepare your paint palette. I am using my favourite edible art paints from Sweet Sticks. As I mentioned in the Tools section on page 27, I've known Miranda (the owner) since both of our businesses were babies, and I now even have a collab range of colours with her. For this cake I have mixed 'Plum', 'Brown' and 'Navy Blue', giving a beautiful deep purple–burgundy which offsets the blue of the ganache.

11. Using a fine paintbrush, go over the pencil lines on the cake with your edible paint.

12. Fill in the detail as you go—don't be afraid to let your creativity shine and go off-script with more detail and shading to create a fuller illustration.

13. I like to rejoin my illustration and keep it on my workbench in case there are some lines that have not transferred visibly enough. If this happens I can look at the printed version and manually add the lines, using the illustration as a reference.

14. Don't overlook the details even if these were not obvious in the original illustration. You want the finished product to be a 'wow' piece from afar, and then as you get closer see more and more detail. Here you can see the beautiful raw-textured edges of the cake, the textured layering of the two-tone ganache and then the details of the illustration.

15. Zoom out, and you have a stunning art piece that wouldn't be out of place in a gallery. You will note that I have positioned the illustration on a diagonal—this ties into my focus of wanting the viewer to be led on a visual journey up the cake. I've stopped the design midway up the middle tier to allow the viewer's eyes to take a break from the detail of the illustration and move up to view the textured edges of the cake before moving on to the textured two-tone ganache and being refreshed by the clean white ganache at the top of the top tier.

LACE STENCIL WITH FRESH FLORALS

TOOLS

pre-prepared cake

Magnolia Kitchen turntable

lace (pre-boiled)

Magnolia Kitchen cake detailing palette knife

ganache (1:4 ratio; see page 254), warmed to a runny/spreadable consistency

Magnolia Kitchen mini metal scraper

florals

greenery

secateurs

florist tape (plastic type)

florist wire

I'm trying to remember how I came up with this lace stencil technique . . . I think it actually started with a piece of baking paper. I was playing around with designs, and I got it into my head that I could ice a cake and then lay a small ripped piece of paper against the icing and ice over it. Once the icing was set I peeled the paper away, and this left an awesome textured ridge design in the icing. Somewhere among all this I had the brainwave to use real lace as a type of stencil— experimenting with this was really fun!

I started incorporating the technique into my designs, and created a similar design to this step-by-step one for the wedding of some of my dearest friends, Jane and Joel. The cake I created for these epic humans was extra special because the lace I used for the stencil was actual lace from Jane's beautiful dress; luckily she is a shorty and I got plenty of offcuts from the hem. It really added an extra element to the design and made it so much more personal and special.

Of course you don't have to go asking your brides to cut up pieces of the dress—you can get offcuts from fabric stores, or use lace trim or even fine lace doilies. Make sure you boil your lace prior to use to ensure that no nasties get transferred onto the cake.

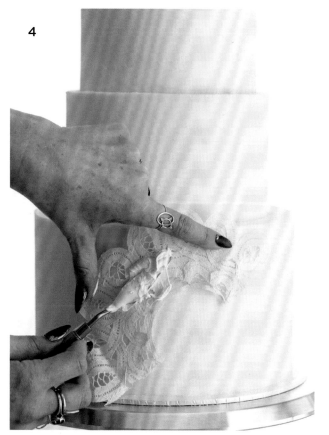

3

6

1. Start with a blank canvas. I have prepped this cake with an uncoloured white chocolate ganache with sharp-as-shit edges.

2. Prepare the ganache you will use for the stencil. I coloured mine white, as I want this design to be subtle against the ivory-yellow colour of the white chocolate ganache already on the cake. The lace design will show white against it.

3. Choose your piece of lace and test the placement by holding it up against the cake. I am using the outer edge of a lace doily that I have trimmed, and also a really fine piece of lace trim that is approx. 10 cm (4 in) wide.

4. Hold the lace in place with your thumb and index finger spread far apart, and use your palette knife to spread a light layer of ganache onto the lace, pushing it against the cake. This first part can be a bit tricky, but it's important to stick the lace to the cake with that first spread of ganache.

5. Add more ganache, spreading it across the piece of lace, covering it entirely and also spreading the ganache off the edge of the lace on to the cake.

6. Using your mini metal scraper, hold it against the cake at a 45-degree angle, press gently and scrap the ganache towards you. You are trying to remove the excess ganache from on top of the lace and smooth the ganache that extends onto the cake over the edges of the lace.

7. After each scrape with the metal scraper, remove the excess ganache using the palette knife. Repeat the scraping motion in step 6 until you have removed all the excess ganache.

8. You can change it up by using multiple different styles of lace. Here I have switched to a finer, more delicate lace, which I have extended up to the second tier at a diagonal, spreading the ganache over the lace and scraping back the same as in steps 4–7.

9. Leave the ganache to set for approx. 5 mins, then gently pull the lace away from the cake.

10. You can rinse the lace in hot water and wring it out in a clean tea towel to re-use. If you are not re-using it for this cake, wash it in the washing machine after rinsing off the ganache and make sure you boil it again before using on a new cake.

11. Here you can see the contrast of the white ganache used for the stencil against the ivory-yellow of the cake itself. The detail of the ganache is showing nicely, and you can also see the ganache that sort of frames the lace stencil.

12. I placed the lace against the cake so that it moved up and over each tier. To do this, simply hold it in place on the top of the tier and spread ganache on the flat top of the tier before holding the rest of the lace against the second tier and following steps 4–7.

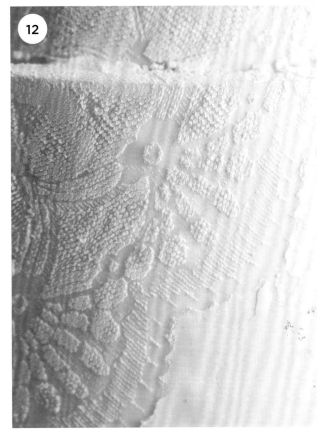

13. Now to move on to the fresh floral part of the design . . . here I only want to add flowers to the top tier, having them spill down from the very top in a diagonal direction. I have chosen a colour palette of yellows and greens. The tools are very basic, but also very important. I prefer the plastic type of florist tape because it provides a full barrier and is also a lot easier to use than the paper types. You just tear off a section and give it a gentle stretch, then cover the end of your stem and begin turning the stem while keeping the tape stretched, gradually working your way up. I like to cover about half of the length of the stem, as this is usually how much will be inserted into the cake.

14. Start by selecting the large flower you want to be the focus for your cluster. Leave about 8–10 cm (3¼ –4 in) of stem on this larger one as it will protrude more from the cake—you will fill in with greenery and filler florals behind and around it. I am using this beautiful green anthurium as my statement flower—honestly, as soon as I spotted it in the florist's I immediately designed the whole cake in my head around this flower.

15. The rest of the flowers I have chosen are mini roses, alstroemeria, chrysanthemums, dried wheat, greenery and some random dangly green thing that reminded me of Sideshow Bob. (I couldn't find the name of it haha so it can just be called Sideshow Bob officially now.)

16. Start filling in around the statement flower. I added some filler slightly underneath and then directly on top of the statement flower. I used Sideshow Bob to cover a lot of the top of the cake. To be honest, he is quite the statement of dangliness all by himself.

19

22

17. Sometimes you will work with flowers that have weak stems which will not hold up to being pushed into the cake, or sometimes they just don't have long enough stems. For these, I trim off the unusable stem and then wire them.

18. To wire a flower, insert florist wire halfway into the base of the flower as shown. The length of the wire should be twice the length of the 'stem' that you want to be able to insert into the cake.

19. Fold the wire in half and twist it slightly so it looks like a braid.

20. Starting with the base of the flower where the wire is inserted, wrap florist tape around and start taping down.

21. Tape the wire all the way down to the bottom.

22. Here is an example of an extended wire stem on a mini rose—all tidy and neat.

23. You can then insert the flower straight into the cake as shown.

24. Keep adding filler flowers until you are happy with how it looks overall—remember to step back every so often and view from a distance, as it gives a different perspective.

25. You can see how I have arranged the florals to spill down the top tier at an angle that follows that of the lace design, so that the lace flows from and extends the florals. Always add enough filler and greenery to disguise where the larger stems are inserted in the cake, even the back of the cake—you never know who will be perving at the back end of your creation!

For a more detailed overview of arranging florals on a cake, see pages 136–145.

25

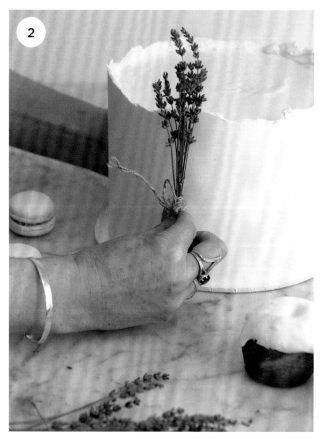

INSTRUCTIONAL
DESSERT SUITE

TOOLS

pre-prepared cake, mini glazed doughnuts and macarons

dried wild lavender

twine

scissors

florist wire

ganache (1:4 ratio; see page 254), at a spreadable consistency

Magnolia Kitchen cake detailing palette knife

paint palette

edible paints

small paint brushes

Designing a cohesive look for multiple desserts can be a great way to give your guests a selection of sweets to feast on alongside the cake. I like to offer this if I have a wedding to quote, as the cake can then be smaller, reducing the cost for the client. Adding desserts that match the cake also means you can cater for larger guest numbers.

There is something pleasing about seeing a dessert suite all set up at an event. It really is a show-stopper—several different desserts designed and decorated to compliment each other. For this instructional I have chosen mini doughnuts, macarons and a single-tiered cake. The design is very simple, but the simplicity is what I feel gives appeal. It's what I call mixed media—I'm using dried wild lavender as a 3D inspiration for the painted lavender. If you don't want to use lavender you could use any type of dried floral—your dessert suite would look amazing with some mini dried roses or even just rose petals arranged on the side of the cake and then some hand-painted petals to match... Ohhhhh now typing that, I want to create another dessert suite! (Just over here inspiring myself while trying to inspire y'all.)

Before you begin, prepare all your desserts. I have prepped my cake with my 'ganache on ganache' technique with raw-textured edges (see page 110), glazed the doughnuts with ganache and filled my macarons. Gather all your tools.

1. Start by gathering a bundle of the lavender and tying it together with the twine.

2. Hold the lavender bundle against the cake—depending on the length of the stems, you may need to trim it to shorten it or even it out neatly. I have chosen to have my lavender bunch stick up over the top of the cake as it adds another dimension and a small amount of height to the single-tier cake.

3. Secure the lavender bundle to the side of the cake with a piece of florist wire formed into a U shape. (See steps 14 and 15 of my Using Fresh Florals instructional on pages 140–141 for more on this.)

4. Make sure your prepared ganache is a spreadable consistency. Using your palette knife, spread a semi-circle of ganache gently onto each macaron top. This should look like a smear of oil paint, to give another texture and level to the design. Place a small sprig of lavender on top of each smear of ganache.

5. Decorate your prepared mini doughnuts with sprigs of lavender as well. Tuck the end of each sprig into the ganache slightly so it stays in place. I am using two longer sprigs for the doughnuts because they are slightly bigger than the macarons and it looks more balanced.

6. Now prepare your paints. I used edible art paints from Sweet Sticks and mixed up custom colours to match the lavender.

7. As I mentioned, this is quite a simple design so don't stress too much about the painting part. Take inspiration from the lavender and just freehand some stalks alongside the bunch of dried lavender flowers. Then add a few abstract dabs of the paint brush from about halfway up each stalk, starting bigger and getting smaller as you move up—again taking inspiration from the lavender. You can paint on as many or as few as you feel like; there are no rules.

8. Here you can see the semi-circle of ganache texture up close on the macaron, which links to the raw-textured edges of the cake—and then of course the lavender to bring all the desserts together as one cohesive design for the dessert table.

9. Using the same style you used on the cake, paint little lavender details onto the ganache doughnuts. Again this ties in the design with both the cake and the macarons.

10. Voilà! How simple was that? I can imagine this dessert suite at an intimate wedding or even a bridal shower. Actually, I can see this design and dessert suite shining at any event—such a great way to celebrate and add variety for your guests.

INSTRUCTIONAL
ICING AND SCRIPTING ON COOKIES

TOOLS

pre-prepared sugar cookies (page 209)

microplane

pre-prepared royal icing (page 212)

spray water bottle

spatula

2 piping bags

scissors

scribe tool or wooden skewer

fine paintbrush

edible paints

prepared script on paper

craft knife

lightbox or window

masking tape

non-toxic pencil

paint palette

Cookies are a great addition to any event—they can be made ahead of time and can be decorated to match any theme. They have been a great love of mine over the years, especially when creating a dessert suite.

I wanted to share this instructional for hand-scripting names onto iced cookies as it is what I actually did for my own wedding! Yes, I iced and hand-decorated over 60 cookies for my big day. Yes, I made the cake too, and yes, I got married at the same time I was opening Magnolia Kitchen Sweet Cafe (the original). YES, I AM A SUCKER FOR A BUSY SCHEDULE.

When it came to planning the guest favours for each place-setting at my wedding, I had a thought that I could kill two birds with one stone. I created all of our own stationery (yes, yes, I did that too) and didn't want to bother with place-settings with our guests' names on them, but of course our guests needed to know where they were seated. So I figured I would create an edible place-setting by way of a cookie.

They were plaque-shaped cookies and they had a burgundy watercolour stripe painted on one side which matched with the hand-dipped paper I had used for our stationery. I hand-painted in gold each of our guests' names, then packaged them in a cellophane bag with a ribbon attached.

They served their purpose AND were delicious! From memory I had flavoured the royal icing with orange oil, and the sugar cookie itself was orange and cardamom. If you have my previous book you will know I am a huge fan of this flavour combo!

Obviously you don't need to script names—you can just have some nice words, or you could paint a picture on the cookies instead. Treat them like a canvas; remember that a lot of the icing techniques in my cake instructionals can also be used on cookies, such as the lace stencil or the oil-paint style. Just use royal icing instead of ganache.

1. Prepare your cookies ready for icing. I like to run my finger around the edges to make sure there are no imperfections . . . if there are any rough bits or sticky-out bits you can use a microplane to shave these off. If you are working with square cookies, the microplane is good for shaving the sides to ensure a perfectly square cookie.

2. Prepare your royal icing for colour and consistency—see the notes below. Use the spatula to scoop each mixture into a piping bag. I am not bothering with icing tips here, as what I am doing is very simple. Seal off the tops of the piping bags—I use a bag clip or a rubber band. You can also just tie a knot in the end if there is enough space.

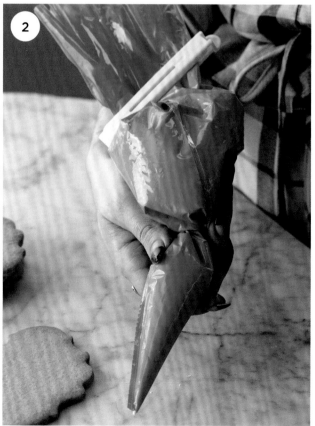

PREPARING ROYAL ICING

See the royal icing recipe (page 212) for more instructions on this subject. For these cookies I am icing first with a flooding consistency and then finishing with a piped border which is a piping consistency.

Measure out the required amount of thick/stiff icing into two separate bowls (one for flooding, one for piping). I used about 160 g (5¾ oz) for the flooding on 20 cookies (see page 215 for how I worked this out). I only need a small amount for the piped border, so maybe just 80 g (3 oz) for the 20 cookies.

Colour (and flavour) these now if required. I have tinted the icing I will flood to a white colour, and am using uncoloured icing for the piped border because I'm going to paint that later.

Mix to the desired consistency:

For flooding consistency, add water (using the spray bottle) a little at a time and stir in. After each addition is combined, drag a spoon through the icing and count slowly. By the time you reach 12, the icing should have settled in on itself and the drag lines from the spoon should have disappeared.

For piping consistency you will only need a very light spray of water—you want the icing to remain stiff, but to settle a little while keeping its shape.

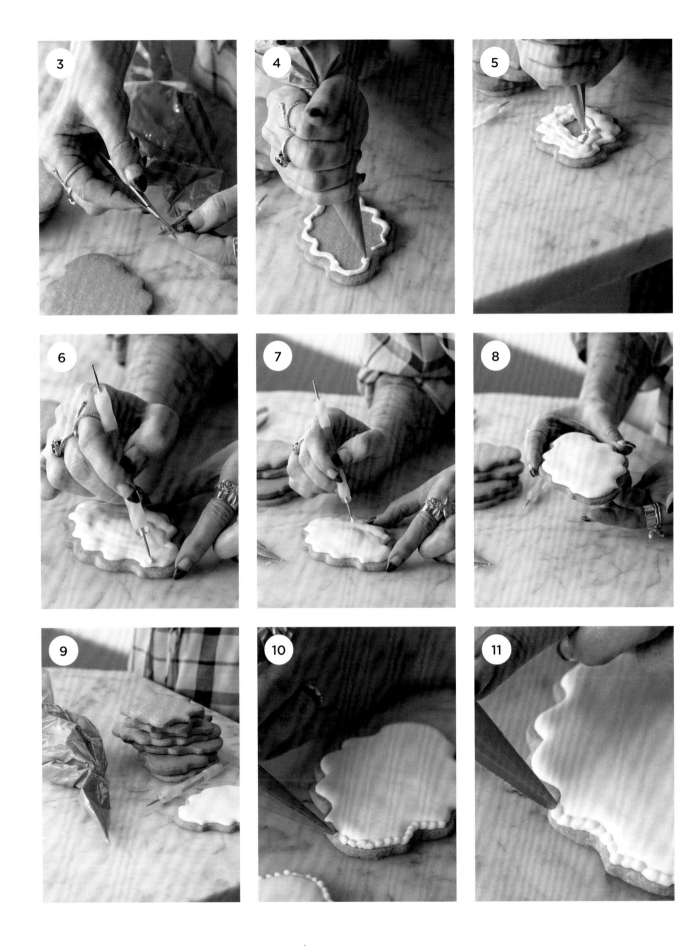

3. Starting with the flooding-consistency icing, snip about 3 mm (⅛ in) off the end of the piping bag. I like to twist the bag about a hand space from the tip. This separates off a manageable, controlled amount of icing so you are not squeezing right from the top, far away from the tip. It is important to have control over the bag. Use one hand to squeeze the bag from the top of the twist, and the other to guide the tip around the cookie.

4. The first step is to pipe a dam around the edge of the cookie, about 2–3 mm (⅛ in) in from the edge. Don't worry if it's not perfect.

5. Then pipe a generous amount of icing inside the dam outline. I like to just pipe another line inside the dam and repeat this until you reach the centre.

6. With your scribe tool or skewer, use circular motions to 'move' the icing around the edges to ensure a tidy edge—this will become easier with practice.

7. Keep going all the way around the icing on the cookie.

8. If your icing is still slightly bumpy and uneven on top of the cookie, you can pick up the cookie gently and, keeping it flat, give it a little jiggle side to side to encourage the icing to settle.

9. Set aside the iced cookie to dry slightly. By the time you have flooded all 20 cookies, the first one will be dry enough to add the outer border.

10. Now you get to use your piping-consistency icing that is already prepped in the piping bag. Snip off about 2–3 mm (⅛ in) from the end of the bag. Holding the piping bag exactly as you did for the flooding, line up the tip of the bag with the edge of the flooded icing and gently squeeze out a small amount of icing so it touches the edge of the icing and sits on the cookie. Squeeze gently, then release and drag the tip of the piping bag gently towards you along the cookie to leave a little dot of icing behind.

11. Place the tip of the icing bag back against the edge of the flooded icing, and repeat step 10 again and again around the edge of the cookie. You want each little dollop of piped icing to be added so that it is touching the little dollop next to it, like a tiny string of pearls.

12. When you get fully around the cookie, your last dollop will just be a dot with no drag. Using a slightly wet, clean paintbrush, gently pat the last dollop so it doesn't have a spike on it. Leave the cookies to dry. They can be dried at room temp overnight on a drying rack, or you can speed up the process by having a fan directed (gently!) onto the cookies. The royal icing needs to be completely set hard prior to painting.

13. Once the icing has fully dried/set, you are ready to add some colour to the border. I want to make it really stand out, so I'm using edible art paint in my Sweet Sticks collaboration colour 'Antique Gold'.

14. For the script, instead of expecting everyone to freehand it, I decided to use the technique in my instructional on cake illustrations (see page 146). I usually open a Word document and type out what I want to write. If I want a custom font I go to a font website like DaFont.com that has free fonts for personal use. You can type in a word and see what it looks like in a range of fonts. I then screenshot my choice and put it in a document where I can resize it.

15. Once you're happy with your names/words, print them and cut out each one separately. Then gather the rest of your tools.

16. For this bit I usually just use a window where there is natural light coming in, but you could also use a lightbox. Turn the paper over so that the printed side is against the window and fix it in place with tape. Using your non-toxic pencil, go over the words. I try to just focus on the main shape of the letters—I can fill in the thickness later.

17. Position your name/words with the pencil side against the cookie, holding it in place with one hand. Make sure your pencil is sharpened, then carefully draw over the letters, pressing lightly so that the pencil on the reverse side transfers onto the cookie. DON'T press so hard that you dig into the cookie and crack the icing! This is why it is important to allow the icing to dry fully.

18. When you have drawn over all the letters, remove the paper to show the light pencil markings on the cookie.

19. I am using edible art paint in 'Black' for the scripting. All you have to do is give the bottle a good shake, put a couple of drops on a paint palette, and use your fine paintbrush to go over the pencil lines that are showing on the cookie. Keep your bit of paper in front of you so that you can copy the thick and thin parts of the scripted font.

20. Done! These are sure to make a delicious statement at your event.

INSTRUCTIONAL
CUTTING AN EVENT CAKE

TOOLS

large, sharp, hot
non-serrated knife

Do you know how to cut a cake?

I'm sure you thought you did, but is it me or are cakes getting taller
and taller these days? Well, you know me—I am all about the tall cakes.
Nothing short and squat about Magnolia Kitchen cakes!

However, the height of an event cake can confuse and befuddle the
person cutting it to serve. Even a single-tier cake can stand about
5–6 inches high (that's 13–15 cm) and have three layers, and it can be
even more confusing when it's a multi-tier cake with a big-ass pole up
the middle.

When I deliver an event cake, I like to include my 'Cake Care
Instructions'. This is a handy-dandy little document I created years
ago. It lets the venue know what the flavours of each tier of the cake
are, and has a handy little drawing of the cake and what the structure
is, including where the various supports are located within the cake
(e.g. centre pole, cake boards, tier supports). I describe the type of icing
and whether it should be refrigerated or can be left at room temperature.
I let them know what needs to be removed from the cake before cutting
and serving (e.g. cake topper, fresh florals, wires).

I know y'all are probably thinking that some of this seems obvious, but
seriously I don't want to be the one dealing with a customer who has
choked on a fresh flower that wasn't removed before serving because
the server didn't know they needed to and nor did the customer who has
scoffed the cake.

The last part of my Cake Care Instructions are specific to the cutting of
the particular event cake.

So. Always start with the top tier USING A LARGE, SHARP, HOT NON-
SERRATED KNIFE, especially if your cake is ganache (as my event
cakes most often are). If you try to cut a ganache-layered cake with a
blunt or serrated or cold knife you will end up dragging the ganache
through the cake layers and it will become a crumbly mess!!

3

6

1. Start with a cake. I'm demonstrating with a three-layer Hummingbird Cake iced sharp-as-shit with cream-cheese-flavoured white chocolate ganache. (Can we just pause to appreciate the perfection of a simple sharp-as-shit cake—all those possibilities, so much potential for design!)

2. HOT knife; HOT NON-SERRATED knife; LARGE SHARP HOT NON-SERRATED knife. When it's hot, wipe it with a clean tea towel so it doesn't leak water all over your beautiful event cake.

3. Starting on one side of the cake, place the knife about 2.5 cm (1 in) from the edge.

4. Cut right through all three layers of cake and icing, and lay the slice off to one side with the icing facing down. This 'end' slice will be heavy on icing; remember there is about 1.25 cm (½ in) of icing surrounding the whole cake.

5. Now that you have removed the mostly-icing part, delight in the beauty of the cake guts.

6. DON'T FORGET TO HEAT YOUR KNIFE AFTER EACH CUT. Repeat steps 3 and 4, cutting straight across the whole cake at spacings of 2.5 cm (1 in).

7. Lie each slab of cake down flat as you go...

8. ...ready to cut into portion sizes.

9. I am starting with a dessert serve, for which I'm being super-anal for teaching purposes and measuring out the 5 cm (2 in) with a ruler. You can find more detail on serve sizes on pages 239–241.

10. Cut down the slab of cake at the right width.

11. You can also cut it into a coffee serve using the ruler (anal teaching purposes) at 2.5 cm (1 in): literally half the size of the dessert serve.

12. Because my cakes are three layers high as standard, a straight cut can make for an excessive serving even if it is a coffee serve. Go ahead and cut the coffee serve in half, and you will have double the amount of serves again.

Remember, don't over-cater your event! Especially if it is a wedding—think about when the cake is likely to be served. Traditionally it is later in the evening when your guests are drunk and are more about 'eating's cheating'.

CUTTING A MULTI-TIERED CAKE
Cut the tiers in situ, starting from the top of the cake and being careful not to cut into the central pole. Cut as described above and shown in the images.

Once the whole top tier is cut, remove the cake board, then start cutting the next tier the same way... repeat until you have cut the entire cake.

7

10

RECIPES

STICKY DATE CARAMEL CAKE

TIMING

CAKE PREP 30 mins

BAKING 30–40 mins

CHILLING 2 hours

MAKES 3 x 18 cm (7 in) round layers

SERVES approx. 18 (dessert-size serves) when decorated

INGREDIENTS

1 recipe Salted Caramel (page 228), pre-prepared

260 g (9¼ oz) pitted dates

2 tablespoons baking soda

500 g (1 lb 2 oz) plain flour

100 g (3½ oz) cornflour (cornstarch)

425 g (15 oz) soft brown sugar

35 g (1¼ oz) baking powder

285 g (10 oz) butter, at room temperature

5 whole eggs

370 g (13 oz) milk

50 g (1¾ oz) canola oil

2 tablespoons date syrup

1½ teaspoons vanilla extract

This cake is proof that dates can be used in something other than a boring-ass scone and can be delicious . . .

Personally dates are not my favourite, which is no disrespect to the date—I just associate childhood trauma with them. Okay, of course that is me being dramatic, but let me explain. My parents owned a health-food shop and my dad was a naturopath, and this meant that when as a child I asked for sweets and candy I would get fucken dried fruit—and the DATE featured a lot as a 'treat' . . . bleugh. I'm definitely standing by my 'childhood trauma' statement. I am well aware of the irony that I now live life by the sweet, sweet sugar crystal and run a business dealing in sugary treats.

METHOD

HAVE YOU PREPARED YOUR CARAMEL?? Come on, I did say 'pre-prepared'.

Preheat your oven to 170°C (325°F). Prepare three 18 cm (7 in) cake tins with cooking spray and line them with baking paper.

Chop your pitted dates, place them in a microwave-safe bowl and cover with boiling water. Sprinkle the baking soda over the dates and microwave in 2-minute bursts until the water has been absorbed. Give it a stir—the dates should fall apart and be mushy. If your dates are not this consistency, add more boiling water and repeat the microwaving step. Set the date mush aside and continue with making the cake batter.

Place all the dry ingredients in the bowl of a stand mixer fitted with the paddle attachment and mix on low speed to combine. Chop your butter into cubes, add it to the dry ingredients and keep mixing on low until the mixture resembles breadcrumbs.

In a separate bowl, mix together the wet ingredients (including the date syrup but NOT THE DATE MUSH) until combined. Add two-thirds of the wet mixture to the dry ingredients and mix on medium-high until thick and fluffy. This step is important for the finished product, so take your fluffiness seriously.

Continued overleaf

To decorate

1.5 kg (3 lb 5 oz) White Chocolate Ganache, 1:4 ratio (page 220)

1 recipe Salted Caramel (page 228)

1 recipe Salted Caramel Ganache (page 227), optional

Add the remaining wet ingredients and mix well until combined and fluffy. Scoop the mixture evenly into the prepared tins (use scales to get them all the same).

Now for the date mush—divide evenly between each tin over the cake batter, then divide your PRE-PREPARED caramel evenly between each tin over the date mush and cake batter. Grab a spoon or stirring implement, and gently fold the date mush and caramel through the cake batter. Don't overfold the cake batter. Look at the picture of this cake—when it's cut open you can see the swirls of date mush and caramel through the baked cake AND DOESN'T IT LOOK EPICLY DELICIOUS? Not a traumatic date vibe in sight!

Now bake for 30–40 mins until the cakes are golden brown and a skewer or knitting needle poked into them comes out clean. Allow to cool in the tins for 5–10 mins, then turn out onto cooling racks.

When the cakes are cool, wrap them in plastic wrap and chill for 2 hours (or overnight)—this will make them easier to trim and ice.

I have iced this cake with White Chocolate Ganache (with a little Salted Caramel mixed through it), and I've used Salted Caramel as a filling between the layers. The top is decorated with piped dollops of Salted Caramel Ganache around the edge, plus more Salted Caramel poured into the middle and spread with a spatula.

EARL GREY CAKE

TIMING

CAKE PREP 1½ hours

BAKING 30–40 mins

CHILLING 2 hours

MAKES 3 x 18 cm
(7 in) round layers

SERVES approx. 18
(dessert-size serves)
when decorated

INGREDIENTS

370 g (13 oz) milk

4 Earl Grey tea bags

500 g (1 lb 2 oz)
plain flour

100 g (3½ oz)
cornflour (cornstarch)

425 g (15 oz) caster
sugar

35 g (1¼ oz) baking
powder

285 g (10 oz) butter,
at room temperature

5 whole eggs

50 g (1¾ oz) canola
oil

1½ teaspoons vanilla
extract

To decorate

1.5 kg (3 lb 5 oz) Earl
Grey Ganache, 1:4
ratio (page 223)

This cake is such an understated flavour, but it's one I find myself indulging in more often than not and is now one of our standard wedding cake taster flavours. I love to educate on flavours that aren't as generic as basic-bitch chocolate or vanilla. If this cake were a lady, she would be as classy as fuck and be at the races wearing a custom pillbox hat with florals on it.

METHOD

Preheat your oven to 170°C (325°F). Prepare three 18 cm (7 in) cake tins with cooking spray and line them with baking paper.

Put your milk in a pot, place it over a medium to low heat and bring to an 'only just boil'—which of course is a made-up Bets-ism. What I mean is that you want your milk to be boiling hot but you don't want it to go all manic and boil over, which it will if you don't remove it from the heat as soon as you see a few little bubbles appear.

Remove the pot from the heat and add your tea bags, then leave to steep for approx. 1 hour. You really want the milk to have a decent strong dark caramel colour to show that the Earl Grey flavour is really infused through.

After your tea has been steeping for about 50 mins you can start prepping your other ingredients.

Place all the dry ingredients in the bowl of a stand mixer fitted with the paddle attachment and mix on low speed to combine. Chop your butter into cubes, add it to the dry ingredients and keep mixing on low until the mixture resembles breadcrumbs.

In a separate bowl, mix together the wet ingredients, including your infused milk . . . do I need to tell you to remove the tea bags?? REMOVE THE TEA BAGS FROM THE MILK, *then* mix the wet ingredients until combined. Add two-thirds of the wet mixture to the dry ingredients and mix on medium-high until thick and fluffy—this step is important for the finished product, so take your fluffiness seriously. Add the remaining wet ingredients and mix well until combined and fluffy.

Scoop the mixture evenly into the prepared tins, using scales to get them all the same.

Continued overleaf

Now bake for 30–40 mins until the cakes are golden brown and when you poke a skewer or knitting needle into them it comes out clean. Allow to cool in the tins for 5–10 mins, then turn out onto cooling racks.

When the cakes are cool, wrap them in plastic wrap and chill for 2 hours (or overnight)—this will make them easier to trim and ice.

I have iced this with my Earl Grey Ganache and decorated it with some dried roses and leaves. If you would like to ice your cake with a sharp-as-shit edge like this, there is an assembly and icing instructional in my first book on pages 68–75.

HUMMINGBIRD CAKE

TIMING

PREP 20 mins

BAKING 30–40 mins

CHILLING 2 hours

MAKES 3 x 18 cm (7 in) round layers

SERVES approx. 18 (dessert-size serves) when decorated

INGREDIENTS

500 g (1 lb 2 oz) plain flour

100 g (3½ oz) cornflour (cornstarch)

425 g (15 oz) caster sugar

35 g (1¼ oz) baking powder

4 teaspoons ground cinnamon

285 g (10 oz) butter, at room temperature

5 whole eggs

320 g (11¼ oz) milk

50 g (1¾ oz) canola oil

1½ teaspoons vanilla extract

400 g (14 oz) can crushed pineapple, drained

2 bananas, mashed

250 g (9 oz) chopped pecans

You may be wondering what a hummingbird cake even is . . . Apart from describing the flavours (which BTW are pretty much all my favourites combined into one delicious cake—more on that in a moment), I figured I would give you a wee history lesson. Because I know y'all love that and because I find it interesting to research the origins of traditional baking styles, techniques and flavours. So, the hummingbird cake is Jamaican! Of course, now that I know this it makes complete sense with the tropical flavours and spice that make up its flavour profile. Apparently it was actually a travel marketing concept to entice international visitors. Don't know about you, but that would totally get me on a plane to Jamaica!

The cake itself is similar to a carrot cake in its moist density, with mashed banana, pineapple, cinnamon and pecans—I mean, to me everything about that is my ideal cake. Traditionally it would be iced with a cream cheese icing which, if you know me, is my weakness—I LOVE CREAM CHEESE. But for this recipe I have chosen a cream cheese 'flavoured' ganache as I wanted a more structural icing to hold the design and be able to sit at room temp.

METHOD

Preheat your oven to 170°C (325°F). Prepare three 18 cm (7 in) cake tins with cooking spray or butter and line them with baking paper.

Place all the dry ingredients in the bowl of a stand mixer fitted with the paddle attachment and mix on low to combine. Chop your butter into cubes, add it to the dry ingredients and keep mixing on low until the mixture resembles breadcrumbs.

In a separate bowl, mix together the eggs, milk, canola oil and vanilla extract. Add two-thirds of this wet mixture to the dry ingredients and mix on medium-high until thick and fluffy. Add the remaining wet mixture and mix well until combined and fluffy.

Add the pineapple, banana and pecans and mix on low until combined.

Continued overleaf

Scoop the mixture evenly into the prepared tins (use scales to get them all the same), and bake for 30–40 mins until the cakes are golden brown and a skewer poked into them comes out clean. Allow to cool in the tins for 5–10 mins, then turn out onto cooling racks.

When the cakes are cool, wrap them in plastic wrap and chill for 2 hours (or overnight)—this will make them easier to trim and ice.

I have iced this in the classic Magnolia Kitchen style with sharp-as-shit edges. The icing is a 1:4 ratio white chocolate ganache flavoured with 2 teaspoons of LorAnn Oils cream cheese flavour (for more detail on ganache ratios see page 254). If you do want to go full traditional, by all means go with the cream cheese icing from my first book—this would be delicious with a touch of cinnamon added to taste.

For decorating I have used some simple dehydrated pineapple slices—before drying them, I coloured them in autumn colours with food colouring. They are such an easy decoration and are in keeping with the flavour of the cake.

MAPLE SAGE AND BROWN BUTTER CAKE

TIMING

CAKE PREP 30 mins

BAKING 30–40 mins

CHILLING 2 hours

MAKES 3 x 18 cm (7 in) round layers

SERVES approx. 18 (dessert-size serves) when decorated

INGREDIENTS

1 recipe Sage-infused Brown Butter (page 232), pre-prepared and at room temperature

500 g (1 lb 2 oz) plain flour

100 g (3½ oz) cornflour (cornstarch)

425 g (15 oz) caster sugar

35 g (1¼ oz) baking powder

10 large sage leaves, finely chopped

5 whole eggs

325 g (11½ oz) milk

50 g (1¾ oz) canola oil

200 g (7 oz) maple syrup

1½ teaspoons vanilla extract

To decorate

1½ recipes Beurre Noisette Buttercream (page 217)

Usually I like to have a wee chat about the recipe before I dive into the ingredients and method, but when it came to this one I realised I'd done all the bloody chit-chatting in the component recipes . . . Classic tangent from me—I got so excited about this cake flavour, but when I realised I was going to need to break it down into component recipes I forgot about the construction recipe here haha. Anyway, I have to say this because my friend Cherie keeps going on about it—she gets credit for inspiring this flavour of cake. Can't wait to see how many times she credits me in her book!

METHOD

Make sure you've prepared your Sage-infused Brown Butter AND LET IT COOL. And keep the sage leaves that you removed from the butter for the decoration.

Preheat your oven to 170°C (325°F). Prepare three 18 cm (7 in) cake tins with cooking spray and line them with baking paper.

Place all the dry ingredients, including your finely chopped sage, in the bowl of a stand mixer fitted with the paddle attachment and mix on low speed to combine. Add your cooled Sage-infused Brown Butter—this will be soft at room temp, so just scoop the lot of it into the dry ingredients and keep mixing on low until the mixture resembles breadcrumbs.

In a separate bowl, mix together the wet ingredients until combined. Add two-thirds of the wet mixture to the dry ingredients and mix on medium-high until thick and fluffy. Don't skimp on the fluffiness— you need it for the best finished product. Then add the remaining wet ingredients and mix well until combined and fluffy again. Scoop the mixture evenly into the prepared tins (use scales to get them all the same).

Bake for 30–40 mins until the cakes are golden brown and a skewer poked into them comes out clean. Allow to cool in the tins for 5–10 mins, then turn out onto plastic wrap and wrap tightly.

Continued overleaf

Place in the fridge to cool for at least 2 hours. This will lock in the moisture and make your cakes nice and chilled when it comes to trimming and icing. Chilled cakes = less crumbliness.

Ice this cake with the Beurre Noisette Buttercream for the full flavour profile I designed. Use the sage leaves that you removed from the infused brown butter to decorate—these are also the best thing I have ever eaten, so maybe make extra as a snack . . . who knew that butter-fried sage leaves could be so tasty?!

For the shoot, I kept the design simple using my raw-textured edge design which you can learn in the instructional on page 111. After stepping back to view the design, I decided to add a second thin layer of vanilla bean Swiss buttercream around the lower third to give an extra dimension to the look. Simple yet effective!

ROASTED PLUM, ROSEMARY AND CREAM CHEESE CAKE

TIMING

PREP 20 mins

ROASTING approx. 40 mins

BAKING approx. 1 hour

COOLING 20 mins in tin

MAKES 1 x 23 cm (9 in) round cake

SERVES approx. 14

INGREDIENTS

Plums

6–8 ripe red plums (or 850 g can whole plums)

4 sprigs of fresh rosemary

120 g (4¼ oz) caster sugar

Cake

400 g (14 oz) plain flour

25 g (1 oz) baking powder

200 g (7 oz) butter, at room temperature

265 g (9¼ oz) caster sugar

1½ teaspoons vanilla extract

360 g (12¾ oz) cream cheese (Philadelphia is best)

4 whole eggs

225 g (8 oz) milk

icing sugar, to dust

This isn't my usual layer-cake iced wonder, but a showstopper nonetheless! Actually you can absolutely use this recipe to create a layered cake as per my usual MO [modus operandi], but for this one I thought it would be a nice 'flop it out of the tin and dust with icing sugar' jobby.

I first made this recipe back in 2018 while holidaying in Tauranga with my 'Baaassttttt Fraaaannnddd' and her family for New Year's. Her neighbour had this laden plum tree out the front of their house and I desperately wanted to create something seasonal using the fruit. I settled on an upside-down-style cake but I wanted to have a serious amount of cream cheese in it too. I don't remember planning to include rosemary in the original flavour profile, but I was also doing a roast onion and garlic dish with these beautiful big fresh rosemary sprigs. My brain went something like this: 'OMG that rosemary smells amazing, ohhhhhhh I wonder if this would go with this plum cream cheese cake . . . ima do it!' So I did it and it was epic.

Fast forward to 2020, and because I'm not the sharpest tool in the shed I had forgotten all about it, plus I'd lost the random piece of paper on which I'd jotted the notes down. So here I am years later re-creating it. (It's pretty much that song from Tenacious D, 'Tribute', where they're singing about the best song in the world but the song they are singing is just a tribute. This recipe is just a tribute to that 2018 New Year's cake that was epic. Honestly, my ability to talk at a tangent knows no bounds.) If plums are out of season, you can use canned plums.

METHOD

Preheat your oven to 170°C (325°F). Grab the tin you will be baking the cake in and line roughly with baking paper.

Continued overleaf

Prepare your plums (I love using fresh Black Doris plums). Cut your plums in half and twist to separate—just leave the stones in as you can remove these after the plums are roasted. Cover the bottom of your tin entirely with plum halves, cut side up, and be generous. If you're using canned whole plums, drain off the liquid before cutting the plums in half and laying them in the bottom of the tin.

Place the fresh sprigs of rosemary in among the plum halves. Sprinkle the sugar over the plums and rosemary and place in the oven to roast for about 40 mins.

While your plums are roasting away in the oven, prep your cake batter. Place the flour and baking powder in a bowl and mix together by hand.

Place the butter, sugar, vanilla and half the cream cheese (180 g/6½ oz) in the bowl of a stand mixer fitted with the paddle attachment and cream together until light and fluffy and well mixed. Add each egg separately, mixing well after each addition and scraping down the sides of your bowl. Add the dry ingredients and mix on low to combine. Add one-third of the milk and mix on medium-high speed until light and fluffy. Add the second third of milk and mix until light and fluffy again, then the last lot and mix until all the milk is incorporated and the mixture is smooth and deliciously fluffy. FYI this is a bowl you will want to lick!

Remove your roasted plums from the oven and carefully remove any stones—use tongs so you don't burn your fingerprints off your fingers. While you're at it, remove the sprigs of rosemary now that their flavour is nicely infused through the plums.

Cut the remaining cream cheese into 2.5 cm (1 in) cubes and arrange in the bottom of the tin among the roasted plums. Spoon your cake batter over the top and spread evenly.

Bake for about 1 hour until the cake is golden and a skewer (or metal knitting needle—if you know, you know) poked into it comes out clean. Allow to cool in the tin for about 20 mins.

To serve, place a platter/plate over the cake tin and flip over, allowing the cake to flop out onto the platter. Remove the baking paper gently so as not to pull the plums away from the batter—there should be extra roasted plum juice that spills down the sides and onto the platter.

This is perfect served with a dusting of icing sugar and dollops of rosemary-infused plum compote and fresh whipped cream.

MINI TARTS

TIMING

DOUGH PREP 15 mins

CHILL/REST at least 30 mins

BAKING approx. 14 mins

FILLING AND TOPPING approx. 1 hour

MAKES 15–20 mini tarts

INGREDIENTS

Tart cases

250 g (9 oz) butter, at room temperature

70 g (2½ oz) icing sugar

½ teaspoon vanilla extract

1 teaspoon vanilla bean paste (equivalent to 1 vanilla pod, scraped)

70 g (2½ oz) cornflour (cornstarch)

260 g (9¼ oz) plain flour

Filling options

Lime Curd (page 231) or Earl Grey Ganache (page 223) or Spiced Caramel (page 228)— or any other filling you like

Meringue topping

100 g (3½ oz) egg whites

200 g (7 oz) caster sugar

These little single-mouthful delights are perfect for events where you want to have a spread of desserts, such as a wedding dessert table. You can add an edible flower to decorate, grab your kitchen flame-thrower and toast the meringue, or just use a touch of gold leaf for elegance. The filling options are endless—try my suggestions below or come up with your own. You could use dark chocolate ganache, salted caramel ganache, plum compote, custard . . .

METHOD

Preheat your oven to 150°C (300°F).

Prepare your tart tray—I use the term 'tart tray' loosely, as I actually use a mini cupcake tray. For reference, the diameter for each tart is 5.5 cm (2¼ in) at the top and 3.5 cm (1⅜ in) at the bottom. Grease the tray holes with cooking spray, then dust with flour, tip the tray upside down and give it a shake/bang to remove any excess flour.

Beat that butter with an electric mixer and the beater attachment until it's soft and fluffy and has lightened in colour by a couple of shades. Turn off your mixer and sieve in your icing sugar, then add both your vanillas and turn your mixer on real slow until the icing sugar is incorporated with the butter. Once it is incorporated, you can turn the mixer up and give it another good beat. Don't just go straight in with your mixer on high—you will get a face full of icing sugar!

Turn the mixer off again and add the cornflour (cornstarch) and plain flour, then mix on low until combined.

Using a mini cookie scoop, portion your dough into your tart tray. If you have a tart tamper, then flour it and squish your dough into the tray holes. These tarts don't need to be perfect, so you can use your thumb to squish the dough in. Push it slightly up the sides of the tray holes and make the top edges semi-even.

Using a fork, give the bottom of each tart a wee stab and place the tray in your preheated oven. Bake for about 14 mins—you don't want to brown these, you just want to cook them enough so they hold their shape once they've cooled.

Continued overleaf

Remove from the oven and allow to cool in the tray for about 5 mins, then chill in the fridge for 20–30 mins. This will make them easier to remove from the tray. I usually place a finger inside each case and gently turn it in the tray ... when it turns, I then pull up and it should slide straight out.

Once you have removed all the cases, set them aside and prepare your fillings. I have prepared Lime Curd for a Key lime pie-inspired tart, Earl Grey Ganache and Spiced Caramel.

Once you have your desired filling, fill the cases to just below the top to allow for the meringue topping. Don't overfill or you'll have a messy overflowing situation on your hands.

To make the meringue topping, place the egg whites and sugar in a heatproof bowl (I do this in my mixer bowl, to save on dishes). Grab a pot that your bowl can rest comfortably on top of. Fill the pot halfway up with water, bring it to the boil then turn down to a simmer.

Put a large spoon in the pot so that steam can escape between the bowl and the pot, then rest your bowl on top of the pot. Stir the mixture in the bowl until the sugar has dissolved into the egg white. To test this, dunk in your thumb and index finger and rub them together—if it feels gritty then leave on the heat longer, if it's smooth then the sugar has dissolved.

Once the sugar is dissolved, transfer to your mixer bowl if you're not already using it. Mix on high using your whisk attachment until stiff peaks are achieved—super STIFF peaks—and your bowl will now be cool to the touch.

Fit a piping bag with a French star tip with an opening size of about 1.5 cm (⅝ in); I use an Ateco #868. Transfer your STIFF meringue into the piping bag and pipe dollops onto your filled tarts. You can serve these tarts with fresh meringue or you can toasty it up!

SUGAR COOKIES

TIMING

PREP 30 mins

CHILLING 15 mins

BAKING approx. 15 mins

INGREDIENTS

400 g (14 oz) plain flour

½ teaspoon salt

½ teaspoon baking powder

1 teaspoon cinnamon (optional)

200 g (7 oz) butter, at room temperature

180 g (6½ oz) caster sugar

40 g (1½ oz) glucose syrup

1 whole egg

This dough can be rolled and stored in the freezer for months . . . then you can get out a sheet of dough as needed. Simply allow it to soften slightly after removing from the freezer, then cut and bake it as normal. Follow the instructional on page 174 to ice them up magnificently.

METHOD

Place the flour, salt, baking powder and cinnamon in a bowl, mix together and set aside.

Put the butter, sugar and glucose syrup in the bowl of a stand mixer fitted with the paddle attachment and beat until the mixture becomes pale and fluffy, scraping down the mixer bowl a couple of times to ensure that all the butter has been beaten in. Add the egg and beat well to combine.

Add the dry ingredients to your mixer bowl and mix on low until the mixture forms a soft dough. Do I need to remind you what happens if you don't MIX ON LOW? The dry ingredients will erupt all over your kitchen!

Prepare four pieces of baking paper about the same size as your baking trays. Divide your dough into two. Roll out one half of the dough between two of the pieces of baking paper until about ½ cm (¼ in) thick. Try to roll the dough into a general rectangle shape. Repeat with the other half of the dough. Place on trays and put them in your fridge to chill for about 15 mins. You can chuck them in the freezer for a faster chill time (about 5 mins) if you're impatient like me.

While the dough is chilling, preheat your oven to 160°C (315°F). Place a clean sheet of baking paper on your baking trays (you'll probably need another two trays). Choose your cookie cutter—you can use whatever shape you want.

Take your cookie dough out of the fridge or freezer and peel off the top layer of baking paper. Push your cutter firmly onto the rolled-out dough until you are sure it has cut cleanly through the chilled dough, then remove the cutter and the cut dough and lay the dough shapes on your lined baking trays, spaced at least a finger-width apart. These don't spread, so don't stress if they seem close.

Continued overleaf

You can re-roll the off-cuts and repeat the chilling and cutting processes. Do NOT add any additional flour—rolling between the sheets of baking paper eliminates the need for 'flouring' to stop sticking.

When they're all done, bake for about 15 mins, until light golden. Remove from the oven and allow to cool on a cooling rack.

FLAVOUR VARIATIONS
- Omit the cinnamon (I did say it was optional).
- Lemon—add ½ teaspoon lemon oil and the zest of 1 lemon.
- Vanilla bean—add ½ teaspoon good-quality vanilla bean paste and 1 teaspoon vanilla extract.
- Ginger—add 1 teaspoon ground ginger.
- Mixed spice—add 1 teaspoon mixed spice.
- Orange and cardamom—add 1 teaspoon ground cardamom, ½ teaspoon orange oil and the zest of 1 orange.
- Chocolate—reduce the flour by 100 g (3½ oz) and replace with 100 g (3½ oz) Dutch cocoa.

ROYAL ICING

TIMING

PREP approx. 10 mins

MAKES approx. 690 g
(1 lb 8 oz)

INGREDIENTS

90 g (3¼ oz)
pasteurised egg
white

500 g (1 lb 2 oz)
icing sugar, sifted

pinch of cream of
tartar

1–2 teaspoons vanilla
extract (to taste)

gel food colour as
required (see notes
overleaf)

Royal icing is one of those icings that's actually quite old-fashioned in the decorating world; however, it has such a relevant place in my kitchen. It's great to use as a 'glue' to stick things to cakes. You can use it for hand-piping decorations on cakes, including little piped flowers. I used royal icing to create the lace effect in the Wedgwood cake design on page 94. It is great on cakes because it sets hard, so your design is safe from smudging and it can easily be painted over once dry.

One of its major uses is for iced cookies (see my instructional on page 174). It is the perfect base for painting and design on cookies, and packages well in cellophane bags without damaging the design or the icing. Don't let the 'sets hard' thing put you off eating it, though—it holds flavour well and on a cookie it always reminds me of those iced animal biscuits we used to get as kids (okay, I didn't get them at home, but when I went to friends' houses I did haha).

METHOD

Add all the ingredients except the colour to the bowl of a stand mixer, and combine by hand (with a spoon) until the mixture is a wet consistency. This will ensure that your icing sugar won't cover every surface in one giant POOF when you turn on your mixer.

Using the whisk attachment, mix on high for 4-ish mins, then switch to the beater attachment and mix for another 1–2 mins on low—this will remove the air bubbles that come from the whisking. The icing will now be a thick, sticky consistency. I like to start with this as it's easier to thin than it is to thicken.

You can store this in the fridge for no longer than 5 days—place it in a container and cover with plastic wrap, making sure the wrap is pushed up against the icing with no air bubbles so that the icing doesn't go crusty. Put an airtight lid on the container too.

When you go to use the icing, you may notice it has separated, with the liquid settling on the bottom of the container. This is normal and it just needs to be remixed by hand, using a spatula, to combine.

Continued overleaf

When you are ready to use your icing, you may need to thin it depending on what you are using it for.

You can use the original thick consistency for piping flowers, as this will give a slight grainy texture to the edges of the flowers and they will hold their shape instantly.

If I am using it to ice cookies (see page 174), I want it to be a 'flooding' consistency. Each cookie will use about ½ tablespoon (8 g/⅓ oz) of thick royal icing, so for 20 cookies I would need around 160 g (5¾ oz).

Water is used to thin the icing. I like to use a spray bottle as it's easier to control how much liquid is being added in small amounts. Usually in cookie-land, royal icing consistencies are talked about as being 10, 15 or 20, which is basically the seconds it takes for the icing to settle in on itself. To work this out, drag a spoon through the icing and start counting how long it takes for the drag mark from the spoon to disappear.

For piping the icing so that the design remains in its form, you want it slightly softer than the stiff icing you made first. Spray a small amount of water onto the amount of thick icing that you've worked out you'll need, and mix to combine. You want the drag mark from the spoon to fully remain but slightly smooth itself.

For flooding I like my icing to be about 12 seconds. This means it won't run off the edge of the cookie but will be runny enough that you can move it around with a scribe tool or wooden skewer and it will settle into a nice flat surface with no peaks.

If you find your icing is too runny, then add more of the thick icing you started with.

NOTES
- Gel is the best for colouring royal icing, as it gives an even colour.
- Always colour your icing in its original thick state, as the gel colour is essentially adding a liquid element to the icing and will naturally thin it slightly.
- For really deep colours, I like to mix the colour the night before because it will deepen over time.
- Flavouring your royal icing is important, and while I have gone with a basic vanilla you can also be more creative. I use LorAnn Oils to flavour royal icing, as a little goes a long way and they don't tend to affect the consistency or colour of the icing. Make sure you add your flavouring at the thick stage, the same as for gel colour.

BEURRE NOISETTE BUTTERCREAM

TIMING

PREP/MIXING
20–30 mins

MAKES approx. 700 g
(1 lb 9 oz)

INGREDIENTS

500 g (1 lb 2 oz)
Brown Butter
(page 232), pre-
prepared and at
room temperature

200 g (7 oz) caster
sugar

90 g (3¼ oz) water

8 egg yolks

1½ teaspoons vanilla
extract

How epicly fancy does the name of this recipe sound? It's French, didn't you know?

When writing this recipe I was on a writers' retreat with old mate Cherie from Pepper & Me . . . we went bush for a couple of days to get some intense writing done. I did mention as we walked into the Airbnb we had booked in Titirangi how amazing our husbands are . . . with just a few days' notice we could escape our lives for some tranquil peace and quiet to write in. Shout-out to Harley and Shannon for being the real MVPs.

Anyway, Cherie mentioned a flavour combo for a savoury recipe—sage and maple butter—and I immediately stole her idea and sweetened it the fuck up by translating it into a flavour combo for a cake. This buttercream is one of three parts of that inspired bush-retreat cake flavour. 'Beurre noisette' means 'a sauce of butter cooked until golden or nut brown' and is such an epic flavour profile to add to baking.

The buttercream itself is a French buttercream, since clearly I have decided to go full French for this recipe. French buttercream uses egg yolk and is made using a similar technique to Italian buttercream, but obviously we are not making a meringue as we do with Italian and Swiss buttercream.

METHOD

Use the Sage-infused Brown Butter recipe on page 232 to pre-prepare this WITHOUT SAGE, and make it ahead of time to allow it to be COMPLETELY COOL. You'll need to make two and a half times the recipe to have enough brown butter.

Place the sugar and water in a pot and heat on medium-high with your thermometer attached.

While the sugar is heating, quickly put your egg yolks in the bowl of your stand mixer and fit the whisk attachment.

Here I've piped Beurre Noisette Buttercream on top of mini banana loaves.

Continued overleaf

Start whipping the egg yolks on high speed immediately, as these take longer to thicken and get fluffy than egg whites. When your sugar syrup reaches 122°C (251°F), remove it from the heat and slowly pour the syrup down the side of the mixer bowl into the whipped yolks while the mixer is going. Allow to beat until the bowl is cool to the touch.

Add the brown butter a spoonful at a time, allowing it to incorporate after each addition. This is similar to its Swiss or Italian buttercream counterparts in that you need to trust the process—if it looks shit, just keep whisking it and trust in the Bets.

When the buttercream has mixed and is beautiful, silky and thick, change from the whisk attachment to the beater attachment. Add your vanilla and mix on low to combine. I like to do this step as it eliminates a lot of the air bubbles that can form from the whisking. Those air bubbles can be a pain in the butt when you're trying to get nice smooth sides on your cake.

Note: I've been baking up a storm testing these recipes and I just ate a piece of the Maple Sage and Brown Butter Cake (page 197) iced with this buttercream—HOLY ACTUAL SHIT! Make this buttercream and that cake NOW!! The balance of sweet from the sugar and savoury from the brown butter is so incredible you just can't understand until it's in your mouth. I rate it as my favourite cake at this moment.

WHITE CHOCOLATE GANACHE

TIMING

PREP/MIXING 30 mins

SETTING 4 hours or overnight

MAKES approx. 1.5 kg (3 lb 5 oz) (for a 1:4 ratio)

INGREDIENTS (1:4 RATIO)

300 g (10½ oz) cream

1200 g (2 lb 10 oz) chopped white compound chocolate

Ganache is what you use when you want to make shit sharp . . . it's all fucken ganache. If you know, you know, right? This is of course my go-to icing—I can make my cake seamless and perfect without needing to cover it in the F word (fondant). Ganache is spreadable at room temperature, it is THE BEST for painting on, and did I mention how good it is for making shit sharp? Like totally sharp-as-shit. And just to be a mind-fuck it makes an epic raw-textured edge too.

Ganache, you are the real MVP.

METHOD

Heat the cream in a pot on your stovetop until it starts to bubble around the edges of the pot—try not to let it boil, as it will burn in seconds.

While the cream is heating, put your chocolate in a heatproof (and preferably microwave-safe) bowl. When the cream is ready, remove it from the heat and pour it directly over the chocolate.

Allow it to rest for approx. 5 mins—this will allow the cream to melt the chocolate. Then use a spatula to stir it together until your ganache resembles a smooth, silky, luscious, chocolatey delight that you could just dive into.

Store the ganache in a bowl or an airtight container at room temperature until you're ready to use it. Always cover it with plastic wrap pushed flat onto the top of the ganache, as this will stop a crusty, crystallised skin forming that can make the ganache taste gritty. I recommend allowing it to set for 4 hours at room temp or preferably overnight.

When it's time to use the ganache, heat it gently in the microwave in bursts: 1 min then stir, 40 secs then stir, 20 secs then stir, then repeat the 20-sec bursts until the ganache is a spreadable consistency.

This 1:4 ratio is perfect for icing a cake. For other ratios and uses, see page 254. See also my note on page 251 about compound chocolate.

EARL GREY GANACHE

Y'all know I love a good coffee, but did you know I am also a tea tippler? Often my husband and I will be sitting on the couch at night and I'll just say 'ttteeeeaaaaa' meaningfully to seemingly no one. This has come to mean 'Babe, can you make me a tea?' Anyway, this ganache is such a GREAT combo and one that is a little more left-field than say a more common espresso chocolate combo. Trust me when I say that the way the dark chocolate brings out the flavour profiles—hints of black tea, a touch of floral and bergamot—is magical.

METHOD

Weigh your cream into your pot and add your tea bags or loose tea. Heat the cream on your stovetop until it starts to bubble around the edges of the pot—you only want a slow boil, so keep an eye on it. For a normal ganache you would remove the cream from the heat at this point, but we want to really infuse the Earl Grey into the cream, so keep it on a low heat without letting it boil for approx. 20 mins.

While the cream is infusing, put your chocolate in a microwave-safe bowl. When your cream is looking like a milky-ass weak tea (light caramel colour), remove it from the heat and discard the tea bags (if using). Pour cream (through a strainer if using loose tea) over your dark chocolate. Leave to rest for approx. 5 mins—this will allow the hot cream to melt the chocolate. Then, stir the cream and chocolate together until it is a beautiful, silky, uniform consistency. While you're there, give it a taste test—you will taste chocolate first, but then pay attention to the developing flavour and aftertaste of the Earl Grey coming through . . .

If your ganache still has lumps of chocolate in it and you're freaking the fuck out, JUST CALM DOWN. Zap your bowl of ganache in the microwave for 20–30 seconds and then give it another stir. That should be enough to melt any remaining chunks. Repeat if necessary. Keep the ganache in the microwave-safe bowl and allow it to set at room temp. Ensure that you cover the ganache with plastic wrap, pushing the plastic wrap against the ganache so no air can get in and make it crusty.

Note: This recipe uses a 1:3 ratio, but you can change the ratio depending on the weather and what you are using the ganache for. For more on ratios and ganache uses see page 254.

MASCARPONE GANACHE

TIMING

PREP/MIXING 20-30 mins

MAKES approx. 750 g (1 lb 10 oz)

INGREDIENTS

250 g (9 oz) mascarpone

500 g (1 lb 2 oz) chopped white chocolate

GLORIOUS, that is what this icing is. True to the 'make shit up as I go along' mantra that I clearly live by, I have developed this simple yet mind-blowingly delicious icing/ filling. I first used it to fill a tiramisu-inspired doughnut, with some Marsala added, and since then I have used it to fill cakes at every opportunity.

METHOD

Weigh out your ingredients into a microwave-safe bowl, then microwave in 30-sec bursts. After each burst, stir well—you will notice the mascarpone starting to melt along with the white chocolate. After approx. 6 bursts, the chocolate will be melted and the mixture will combine and become a beautiful silken goddess.

You can use this immediately as a glaze, or cover it with plastic wrap and allow it to set at room temp until desired consistency is reached. When you cover it, ensure that you push the plastic wrap against the top of the ganache so no air can get to it. If it is not covered like this and air gets in, your ganache will set on top and get crusty, then those crusty bits will get mixed through your beautiful silky goddess ganache and it will become gritty and yuk.

This can be used as is with no additional flavouring, or check out some of my flavour inspos below.

VANILLA BEAN MASCARPONE GANACHE

After the ganache is made, add 1 teaspoon vanilla extract and ¼ teaspoon vanilla bean paste, and stir through until fully incorporated.

MARSALA MASCARPONE GANACHE

After the ganache is made, add 35 g (1¼ oz) Marsala (Sicilian fortified wine), and stir through until fully incorporated. Great with espresso desserts and dustings of Dutch cocoa (*hint hint* tiramisu flavour profiles).

SPICED PUMPKIN MASCARPONE GANACHE

After the ganache is made, add 130 g (4¾ oz) pumpkin purée (I use Libby's brand) and ¾ teaspoon mixed spice, and stir through until fully incorporated. This was inspired by Thanksgiving and pumpkin pie—go on, be adventurous.

SALTED CARAMEL GANACHE

TIMING

PREP/MIXING approx. 60 mins

MAKES approx. 600 g (1 lb 5 oz)

INGREDIENTS

225 g (8 oz) caster sugar

120 g (4¼ oz) cream

90 g (3¼ oz) butter, cubed

2 teaspoons Marlborough sea salt flakes

230 g (8 oz) chopped white chocolate

Yes, yes, I know y'all have seen a few of the recipes in this section before, and no, I'm not being a lazy bitch and recycling recipes, I am actually being helpful and have done this for your convenience so you don't have to flick back and forth between books. You're welcome haha.

METHOD

Put a deep pot over a low heat. Sprinkle one-third of the sugar in an even layer over the bottom of the pot and let it start to melt, then add another third of the sugar, gently stir into the melted sugar and allow to melt again. Repeat with the remaining sugar and heat until it is completely liquid and starts to turn an amber colour. DO NOT LEAVE THE KITCHEN—it will burn in seconds.

While the sugar is caramelising, put the cream in a microwave-safe bowl and heat in your microwave for about 2 mins on high, or until hot. When the caramel is an amber colour and all the sugar has dissolved, remove it from the heat. While whisking, slowly add the cream to the caramel and keep whisking to combine—be very careful, 'cause this will bubble up like a witch's cauldron and it can spit.

Whisk until the cream and caramel have combined nicely. If you find that the caramel has slightly seized and there are chunks of gooey caramelised sugar in there, put the pot back over a low heat and keep whisking until it is all combined.

Off the heat, add the butter and stir with the whisk until it's melted, then use an electric hand-held beater to beat the caramel until the butter has completely emulsified and the caramel is silky and smooth. Sprinkle in the salt and stir through with a spoon.

Transfer the hot salted caramel straight to the metal bowl of your stand mixer with the paddle attachment fitted. Add the white chocolate and beat on low speed until fully combined.

Note: If your ganache is very oily or even separated when you combine the chocolate and hot caramel, THIS IS EASILY FIXED SO DON'T PANIC. Just splash in some cold cream (approx. 30 ml/1 fl oz) and combine completely.

Here I've filled two Sugar Cookies (page 209) with Beurre Noisette Buttercream (page 217) and piped dollops of Salted Caramel Ganache on top. Then I've scattered over Valrhona crunchy pearls in 55% dark chocolate and 32% Dulcey (blond chocolate).

SPICED OR SALTED CARAMEL

PREP/MIXING approx. 60 mins

MAKES approx. 400 g (14 oz)

INGREDIENTS

Basic caramel

225 g (8 oz) caster sugar

120 g (4¼ oz) cream

90 g (3¼ oz) butter, cubed

For Spiced Caramel version

¼ teaspoon ground cardamom

¼ teaspoon ground nutmeg

¼ teaspoon ground ginger

½ teaspoon ground cinnamon

pinch of ground cloves

½ teaspoon good-quality vanilla bean paste

For Salted Caramel version

2 teaspoons Marlborough sea salt flakes

Liquid gold, the nectar of the gods . . . sometimes I forget how divine this stuff is and then I'll be making some and I'll lick the spoon and my mind will blow all over again at the deliciousness! Make the spiced version too—trust me, it's a game changer.

METHOD

Put a deep pot over a low heat. Sprinkle one-third of the sugar in an even layer over the bottom of the pot and let it start to melt, then add another third of the sugar, gently stir into the melted sugar and allow to melt again. Repeat with the remaining sugar and heat until it is completely liquid and starts to turn an amber colour. DO NOT LEAVE THE KITCHEN—it will burn in seconds.

While the sugar is caramelising, put the cream in a microwave-safe bowl and heat in your microwave for about 2 mins on high, or until hot. When the caramel is an amber colour and all the sugar has dissolved, remove it from the heat. While whisking, slowly add the cream to the caramel and keep whisking to combine—be very careful as it will bubble up like crazy and spit at you like a feral cat.

Whisk until the cream and caramel have combined nicely. If the sugar seizes slightly and you have chunks of gooey caramelised sugar in there, put the pot back over a low heat and keep whisking until it is all combined.

Take the pot off the heat, add the butter and stir with the whisk until it's melted, then use an electric hand-held beater to beat the caramel until the butter has completely emulsified and the caramel is silky and smooth.

Up until here, the recipes are the same. Now, for Spiced Caramel add the spices and vanilla paste and stir through with a spoon. For Salted Caramel, sprinkle in the salt and stir through likewise.

Pour into a heatproof jar and allow to cool completely before using. DO NOT scrape out the pot while it's still hot and lick the spoon—you will get third-degree burns.

LIME CURD

TIMING

PREP 5–8 mins

COOKING 30–40 mins

MAKES approx. 500 g
(1 lb 2 oz)

INGREDIENTS

160 g (5¾ oz) lime juice

1 tablespoon lime zest

85 g (3 oz) butter, at room temperature

2 egg yolks

2 whole eggs

220 g (7¾ oz) caster sugar

This recipe is one of those 'if you know, you know' things. I say that because when I released my first book with my curd recipe that basically goes against every rule and every teaching on how to make curd IT BLEW YOUR MINDS. To this day I get messages about how it has become a staple in people's kitchens because it is EASY AS FUCK to make and because of course it is DELICIOUS AS FUCK.

So now we are doing a lime curd, and this is my favourite of the citruses. Come on and join the 'if you know, you know' Magnolia Kitchen curd club.

METHOD

Place all the ingredients in a blender (I find a smoothie blender is best), and blend on high speed until combined.

Pour into a pot and heat on low, stirring occasionally. Your curd will begin to produce large, slow-popping bubbles. By this stage it will have thickened. Remove it from the heat, transfer it to a clean jar, allow to cool and store in the fridge. It should keep for a couple of weeks, but the rule of thumb is don't eat it if it's got mould growing on it.

SAGE-INFUSED BROWN BUTTER

TIMING

COOKING 5-10 mins

MAKES approx. 200 g
(7 oz)

INGREDIENTS

10 fresh sage leaves

300 g (10½ oz)
salted butter, roughly
cubed

*While this recipe is destined for sweet sweet sweet, it is
also an EPIC base for fried gnocchi! Or leave out the sage
and just keep a good stock of brown butter in the fridge for
other baking—replace basic-bitch butter in a recipe with
this next-level nutty-depth-of-flavour brown butter.*

*I am OBSESSED—I was literally eating this butter straight
out of the bowl it was cooling in . . . actually dipping my
finger into it as soon as it had set and eating it. DO NOT
JUDGE ME.*

METHOD

Before you start—are you using this for one of my other recipes or for a
recipe that requires a specific quantity of finished brown butter? If it's
for another recipe, keep in mind how much you need, as the amount of
brown butter you get is quite a bit less than the amount of butter you
started with. When making the brown butter, some of the water content
of the butter will evaporate so you will lose some of the weight in the
cooking process.

For this it is best to use a light-coloured pot or deep frying pan so you
can see the colour of the butter change. This is the fastest cook in the
history of time, so don't diddle around or walk away from the stove—it
will go from brown butter to black butter in the space of 20 seconds.

Crush your sage leaves by smooshing them between the palms of your
hands and twisting gently; this will release the aromatics from the leaf.
Now chuck 'em in the pot.

Add the butter and mix together with the sage on a low to medium heat.
When the butter is fully melted and looks a little bubbly and frothy, turn
the heat to low. The milk solids will be at the bottom of the pan and this
is what you are browning. Move the butter around with a wooden spoon
so you can keep an eye on the milk solids colour. The darker the colour,
the nuttier the taste.

When it reaches a light brown colour, remove from the heat—it will keep
browning after it's removed, so it is important to remove it at this lighter
brown stage.

Continued overleaf

Using a fork or tongs, remove the pieces of sage leaves and set aside on a paper towel. These can be used to decorate cakes, or seriously just snack on them—THEY ARE FREAKEN DELICIOUS, like INSANELY EPIC! Like a godly version of kale chips!

Transfer to a heatproof bowl and allow to cool completely before using in the cake/buttercream recipes.

Here's my technique for cooling because I think this will be hugely helpful. Allow to cool slightly on the bench, then move it to the fridge. When your butter starts to solidify around the outside and across the bottom, stir it together and leave to chill some more. When it reaches a consistency where it's half solid bits and half liquid, remove it from the fridge and use a stick blender to blend it together until smooth. It will lighten in colour, too. It should be the consistency of very soft room-temp butter, and will have speckles of the browned milk solids through it which give it the nutty flavour. GO ON—SMELL IT!

Store the butter in a container or jar at room temp. If it is summer, you may need to store it in the fridge as you would normal butter. Allow it to come to room temp before using.

CALCULATIONS AND SCALING

A NOTE ABOUT MEASUREMENTS

———

Okay, let's get this out of the way first.

I AM A METRIC GIRL—grams are the only way to bake, okay?! Don't message me and ask me to convert my recipe to cups for you, 'cause I WILL NOT DO IT and will instead encourage you to join the gram club. Baking requires accurate measurement of ingredients, which you can't achieve when a recipe says 'scant cup' or even cup in general, since the cup measurement, as we know, differs from country to country. GO WITH THE GRAMS FOR SUCCESS. (Also see my notes about scales on page 20.)

BUT (and yes, there is a but, and it pains me as I feel like it makes my metric status seem weaker . . .), when it comes to cake sizes and serves I'm all about those inches—which *yes, yes I know* are imperial units, but just go with it okay? I don't have a really logical reason like I do with grams for weighing, other than it's just how we do it in the cake world. IT JUST IS.

Cake tins across the globe are almost always described in inches; cake boards/cards—INCHES; height of cakes—INCHES; serving sizes—INCHES. Look at it this way: 2.5 cm × 2.5 cm for a coffee serve is four characters more to type than 1 in × 1 in, and inches can also be abbreviated to a simple " (double quote mark), so 1" × 1".

When it comes to scaling recipes, grams are just better and easier to scale, so unless we are talking about cake size we are all about the gram life. OKAY!

Here's a useful little table for those of you who grew up with metric and aren't yet used to inches.

CENTIMETRES	INCHES
2.5	1
5	2
7.5	3
10	4
13	5
15	6
18	7
20	8
23	9
25	10

CALCULATING SERVES

Sometimes it can be difficult to guess how many people a cake is going to serve. Without fail, people ALWAYS over-cater events and there is often so much food wastage! The last thing a baker wants to hear is that 'there was so much cake left over'.

As a baker, I don't want my customers to pay for something they are not going to be able to eat, so I always recommend *under-catering* for cake. Remember, there are people who can't eat cake, there are people who won't eat cake (seriously—who *are* these people and why are they like this?!) and there will likely be guests (especially at a wedding) who will be too wasted to eat cake.

Take into consideration the height of a cake—all standard Magnolia Kitchen cakes are three layers. Some of our customers will choose to serve each portion cut in half so it is only 1½ layers of cake. This is an alternative way to divide it up while still ensuring that everyone gets a fair-sized piece of cake. (Of course, if you and your guests are cake fiends or you actually just want to live on cake for the week after your event, then by all means over-cater!)

At Magnolia Kitchen we use the following serving sizes:
- DESSERT SERVE: a rectangular portion, 2 in × 1 in
- COFFEE SERVE: a square portion, 1 in × 1 in (half a dessert serve)

The following table shows the approximate number of serves you will get from a single-tier (three-layer) cake, depending on its size.

	ROUND		SQUARE	
	Dessert serve	Coffee serve	Dessert serve	Coffee serve
	2 in x 1 in	1 in x 1 in	2 in x 1 in	1 in x 1 in
4 in	6	12	8	16
5 in	9	18	12	24
6 in	14	28	18	36
7 in	18	36	24	48
8 in	26	52	32	64
9 in	30	60	40	80
10 in	38	76	50	100

If you need more than a single tier for your event, simply add the serves from each tier together. So:

Three tiers of 9 in + 7 in + 5 in will make approximately:
30 + 18 + 9 = 57 dessert serves, or
60 + 36 + 18 = 114 coffee serves

SCALING MAGNOLIA KITCHEN CAKE RECIPES

The following calculations are based on Magnolia Kitchen recipes and are specific to each cake being round and having three layers per recipe. If you are only wanting a single layer, divide the recipe by 3; and if you only want two layers, divide the recipe by 3 then multiply by 2.

Remember, I weigh everything in grams, including liquids—it's just easier, and what makes my life easier makes your life easier. For more tips on equipment, ingredients and for general pearls of wisdom see pages 20–25. Some of this info you will have seen in my previous book, but it's equally relevant and helpful in this book.

On the following pages I have scaled four of my cake recipes from my first book. On the left is the method; on the right, the scaled ingredient amounts depending on the size of cake required. Note that the vanilla cake recipe in my first book has multiple flavour variations, so if you are making one of these variations you will also need to manually scale the additional ingredients within that recipe. I've explained how to do this beside the vanilla cake scaling chart.

A Magnolia Kitchen dessert serve (2 in wide x 1 in deep) alongside a Magnolia Kitchen coffee serve (1 in wide x 1 in deep). These have been cut from a single three-layer cake. You could also make a coffee serve by slicing the dessert serve in half through the middle so it is only 1½ layers.

METHOD FOR MAGNOLIA KITCHEN SIGNATURE RICH CHOCOLATE CAKE

Preheat your oven to 170°C (325°F). Prepare three cake tins with cooking spray or butter and line with baking paper.

Place the flour, sugar, cocoa and baking soda in the bowl of a stand mixer fitted with the paddle attachment, and mix on low to combine. Add the butter and mix on low until the mixture resembles breadcrumbs. (You could do this by hand, but really the stand mixer is the way to go.)

In a separate bowl, dissolve the instant coffee in the warm water (or just use the shot of espresso, then add the water). Add the eggs, oil and vanilla and mix together. Add two-thirds of the wet mixture to the dry ingredients and mix on medium-high until thick and fluffy.

Add the remaining wet ingredients and mix well until combined and the batter is smooth. Make sure you scrape down the bowl and then continue mixing, as the dry mixture can get stuck at the bottom and you really want a nice, smooth consistency.

Add the buttermilk and mix slowly to combine. There may be small chunks of buttermilk but don't fret, this is normal. This batter is quite wet, so don't panic if it's not thick.

Pour the mixture evenly into the prepared tins (use your scales to get them all the same weight, as this will make them even heights once baked). Bake for 30–40 mins until a skewer or knitting needle poked into the cakes comes out clean. Allow to cool in the tins for 5–10 mins, then turn out onto cooling racks.

When the cakes are cool, wrap them in plastic wrap and chill for 2 hours or overnight—this will make them easier to trim and ice.

MAGNOLIA KITCHEN SIGNATURE RICH CHOCOLATE CAKE

The 7-in recipe is the control size

4 & 5 in	½ recipe	approx. 1170 g	6 in	¾ recipe	approx. 1750 g
183	grams	plain flour	274	grams	plain flour
300	grams	soft brown sugar	450	grams	soft brown sugar
60	grams	Dutch cocoa	90	grams	Dutch cocoa
8	grams	baking soda	11	grams	baking soda
125	grams	butter (room temp)	188	grams	butter (room temp)
0.5	teaspoon	instant coffee	0.75	teaspoon	instant coffee
or 15	grams	espresso	or 23	grams	espresso
185	grams	warm water	278	grams	warm water
2		whole eggs	3		whole eggs
60	grams	canola oil	90	grams	canola oil
1	teaspoon	vanilla extract	1.5	teaspoons	vanilla extract
130	grams	buttermilk	195	grams	buttermilk
7 in	**1 recipe**	**approx. 2330 g**	**8 in**	**1¾ recipes**	**approx. 4080 g**
365	grams	plain flour	639	grams	plain flour
600	grams	soft brown sugar	1050	grams	soft brown sugar
120	grams	Dutch cocoa	210	grams	Dutch cocoa
15	grams	baking soda	26	grams	baking soda
250	grams	butter (room temp)	438	grams	butter (room temp)
1	teaspoon	instant coffee	1.75	teaspoons	instant coffee
or 30	grams	espresso	or 53	grams	espresso
370	grams	warm water	648	grams	warm water
4		whole eggs	7		whole eggs
120	grams	canola oil	210	grams	canola oil
2	teaspoons	vanilla extract	3.5	teaspoons	vanilla extract
260	grams	buttermilk	455	grams	buttermilk
9 in	**2 recipes**	**approx. 4660 g**	**10 in**	**2½ recipes**	**approx. 5830 g**
730	grams	plain flour	913	grams	plain flour
1200	grams	soft brown sugar	1500	grams	soft brown sugar
240	grams	Dutch cocoa	300	grams	Dutch cocoa
30	grams	baking soda	38	grams	baking soda
500	grams	butter (room temp)	625	grams	butter (room temp)
2	teaspoons	instant coffee	2.5	teaspoons	instant coffee
or 60	grams	espresso	or 75	grams	espresso
740	grams	warm water	925	grams	warm water
8		whole eggs	10		whole eggs
240	grams	canola oil	300	grams	canola oil
4	teaspoons	vanilla extract	5	teaspoons	vanilla extract
520	grams	buttermilk	650	grams	buttermilk

METHOD FOR BASIC VANILLA BEAN CAKE

Preheat your oven to 170°C (325°F). Prepare three cake tins with cooking spray or butter and line them with baking paper.

Place all the dry ingredients in the bowl of a stand mixer fitted with the paddle attachment and mix on low to combine. Chop your butter into cubes, add it to the dry ingredients and keep mixing on low until the mixture resembles breadcrumbs. (You could do this by hand, but really, go buy a stand mixer—it will be worth it.)

In a separate bowl, mix together the wet ingredients (including both vanillas) until combined. Add two-thirds of the wet mixture to the dry ingredients and mix on medium-high until thick and fluffy. Add the remaining wet ingredients and mix well until combined and, yes, FLUFFY.

Scoop the mixture evenly into the prepared tins (use scales to get them all the same) and bake for about 30 mins until the cakes are golden brown and a skewer poked into them comes out clean. Allow to cool in the tins for 5–10 mins, then turn out onto cooling racks.

When the cakes are cool, wrap them in plastic wrap and chill for 2 hours (or overnight)—this will make them easier to trim and ice.

HOW TO SCALE FLAVOUR-VARIATION INGREDIENTS

Do this according to the number of eggs in the control size. For example, the 7-inch vanilla bean cake is the control size and this has 5 eggs. A 4-inch vanilla bean cake has 2 eggs. To make a 4-inch coconut cake as a variation of the basic vanilla bean cake, follow this calc:

150 g coconut ÷ 5 = 30 g (so it's this much coconut per egg)
30 g × 2 = 60 g coconut for a 4-inch cake with 2 eggs

BASIC VANILLA BEAN CAKE

The 7-in recipe is the control size

4 in	⅖ recipe	approx. 810 g	5 in	⅗ recipe	approx. 1210 g
200	grams	plain flour	300	grams	plain flour
40	grams	cornflour/cornstarch	60	grams	cornflour/cornstarch
170	grams	caster sugar	255	grams	caster sugar
14	grams	baking powder	21	grams	baking powder
114	grams	butter (room temp)	171	grams	butter (room temp)
2		whole eggs	3		whole eggs
148	grams	milk	222	grams	milk
20	grams	canola oil	30	grams	canola oil
0.6	teaspoon	vanilla extract	0.9	teaspoon	vanilla extract
0.4	teaspoon	vanilla bean paste	0.6	teaspoon	vanilla bean paste
6 in	**⅘ recipe**	**approx. 1620 g**	**7 in**	**1 recipe**	**approx. 2020 g**
400	grams	plain flour	500	grams	plain flour
80	grams	cornflour/cornstarch	100	grams	cornflour/cornstarch
340	grams	caster sugar	425	grams	caster sugar
28	grams	baking powder	35	grams	baking powder
228	grams	butter (room temp)	285	grams	butter (room temp)
4		whole eggs	5		whole eggs
296	grams	milk	370	grams	milk
40	grams	canola oil	50	grams	canola oil
1.2	teaspoons	vanilla extract	1.5	teaspoons	vanilla extract
0.8	teaspoon	vanilla bean paste	1	teaspoon	vanilla bean paste
8 in	**1⅕ recipes**	**approx. 2420 g**	**9 in**	**1⅗ recipes**	**approx. 3230 g**
600	grams	plain flour	800	grams	plain flour
120	grams	cornflour/cornstarch	160	grams	cornflour/cornstarch
510	grams	caster sugar	680	grams	caster sugar
42	grams	baking powder	56	grams	baking powder
342	grams	butter (room temp)	456	grams	butter (room temp)
6		whole eggs	8		whole eggs
444	grams	milk	592	grams	milk
60	grams	canola oil	80	grams	canola oil
1.8	teaspoons	vanilla extract	2.4	teaspoons	vanilla extract
1.2	teaspoons	vanilla bean paste	1.6	teaspoons	vanilla bean paste
10 in	**2 recipes**	**approx. 4040 g**			
1000	grams	plain flour			
200	grams	cornflour/cornstarch			
850	grams	caster sugar			
70	grams	baking powder			
570	grams	butter (room temp)			
10		whole eggs			
740	grams	milk			
100	grams	canola oil			
3	teaspoons	vanilla extract			
2	teaspoons	vanilla bean paste			

METHOD FOR CARROT CAKE

Preheat your oven to 180°C (350°F). Prepare three cake tins with cooking spray or butter and line them with baking paper.

Whisk the eggs in your stand mixer on high speed until pale and fluffy. Change to the paddle attachment, add the remaining ingredients and mix to combine. Scoop the mixture evenly (use scales) into the prepared tins. Bake for about 35 mins, until the cakes are golden brown and a skewer poked into them comes out clean(ish)—I say 'ish' because carrot cake is very dense, and so the skewer will often not be completely clean when you test the cake. What you *don't* want to see on the skewer is wet or raw batter.

Carrot cake always ends up with an annoying big dome in the middle, so lay a clean tea towel over the top of each cake as soon as you remove it from the oven and press down firmly on the dome to flatten it out. Trust me, this does *not* damage the cake and will do away with that pesky dome. Allow to cool in the tins for 5–10 mins, then turn out onto cooling racks.

When the cakes are cool, wrap them in plastic wrap and chill for 2 hours or overnight—this will make them easier to trim and ice.

CARROT CAKE

The 5-in recipe is the control size

4 in	⅔ recipe	approx. 1000 g	5 in	1 recipe	approx. 1500 g
2		whole eggs	3		whole eggs
83	grams	canola oil	125	grams	canola oil
200	grams	plain flour	300	grams	plain flour
150	grams	caster sugar	225	grams	caster sugar
10	grams	baking soda	15	grams	baking soda
7	grams	ground cinnamon	10	grams	ground cinnamon
267	grams	grated carrot	400	grams	grated carrot
113	grams	crushed pineapple	170	grams	crushed pineapple
67	grams	chopped walnuts	100	grams	chopped walnuts
6 in	**1⅓ recipes**	**approx. 2000 g**	**7 in**	**1⅔ recipes**	**approx. 2500 g**
4		whole eggs	5		whole eggs
167	grams	canola oil	208	grams	canola oil
400	grams	plain flour	500	grams	plain flour
300	grams	caster sugar	375	grams	caster sugar
20	grams	baking soda	25	grams	baking soda
13	grams	ground cinnamon	17	grams	ground cinnamon
533	grams	grated carrot	667	grams	grated carrot
227	grams	crushed pineapple	283	grams	crushed pineapple
133	grams	chopped walnuts	167	grams	chopped walnuts
8 in	**2⅓ recipes**	**approx. 3500 g**	**9 in**	**3 recipes**	**approx. 4500 g**
7		whole eggs	9		whole eggs
292	grams	canola oil	375	grams	canola oil
700	grams	plain flour	900	grams	plain flour
525	grams	caster sugar	675	grams	caster sugar
35	grams	baking soda	45	grams	baking soda
23	grams	ground cinnamon	30	grams	ground cinnamon
933	grams	grated carrot	1200	grams	grated carrot
397	grams	crushed pineapple	510	grams	crushed pineapple
233	grams	chopped walnuts	300	grams	chopped walnuts
10 in	**4 recipes**	**approx. 6000 g**			
12		whole eggs			
500	grams	canola oil			
1200	grams	plain flour			
900	grams	caster sugar			
60	grams	baking soda			
40	grams	ground cinnamon			
1600	grams	grated carrot			
680	grams	crushed pineapple			
400	grams	chopped walnuts			

METHOD FOR RED VELVET CAKE

Preheat your oven to 180°C (350°F). Prepare three cake tins with cooking spray or butter and line them with baking paper.

Place the flour, sugar and cocoa in the bowl of a stand mixer fitted with the paddle attachment and mix on LOW to combine. (Note that if you accidentally put it on high you'll end up with a face full of flour and cocoa.) Chop your butter into cubes, add it to the dry ingredients and mix on low until the mixture resembles breadcrumbs. (You can do this by hand, but seriously, use a stand mixer!)

In a separate bowl, mix together the eggs, buttermilk and food colour—don't forget to *oooh* and *ahhhhh* at the pretty colour. Add two-thirds of the buttermilk mixture to the mixer bowl and mix on medium-high until combined. Add the remaining buttermilk mixture and mix well until combined and the batter is fluffy and a light burgundy colour.

Combine the cider vinegar and baking soda—just like in science class, this will bubble up. Add your bubbly soda to the batter and mix on low to combine. Scoop the mixture evenly into the prepared tins (use your scales) and bake for approx. 30 mins, until a skewer poked into the cakes comes out clean. Allow to cool in the tins for 5–10 mins, then turn out onto cooling racks.

When the cakes are cool, wrap them in plastic wrap and chill for 2 hours (or overnight)—this will make them easier to trim and ice.

RED VELVET CAKE

The 6-in recipe is the control size. For 12 mini cakes, use ⅓ recipe

4 in	⅓ recipe	approx. 570 g	5 in	⅔ recipe	approx. 1130 g
150	grams	plain flour	300	grams	plain flour
150	grams	caster sugar	300	grams	caster sugar
30	grams	cocoa powder	60	grams	cocoa powder
65	grams	butter (room temp)	130	grams	butter (room temp)
1		whole egg	2		whole eggs
120	grams	buttermilk	240	grams	buttermilk
0.5	teaspoon	red gel food colour	1	teaspoon	red gel food colour
2	teaspoons	cider vinegar	4	teaspoons	cider vinegar
1	teaspoon	baking soda	2	teaspoons	baking soda
6 in	**1 recipe**	**approx. 1700 g**	**7 in**	**1⅔ recipes**	**approx. 2830 g**
450	grams	plain flour	750	grams	plain flour
450	grams	caster sugar	750	grams	caster sugar
90	grams	cocoa powder	150	grams	cocoa powder
195	grams	butter (room temp)	325	grams	butter (room temp)
3		whole eggs	5		whole eggs
360	grams	buttermilk	600	grams	buttermilk
1.5	teaspoons	red gel food colour	2.5	teaspoons	red gel food colour
6	teaspoons	cider vinegar	10	teaspoons	cider vinegar
3	teaspoons	baking soda	5	teaspoons	baking soda
8 in	**2 recipes**	**approx. 3400 g**	**9 in**	**2⅔ recipes**	**approx. 4530 g**
900	grams	plain flour	1200	grams	plain flour
900	grams	caster sugar	1200	grams	caster sugar
180	grams	cocoa powder	240	grams	cocoa powder
390	grams	butter (room temp)	520	grams	butter (room temp)
6		whole eggs	8		whole eggs
720	grams	buttermilk	960	grams	buttermilk
3	teaspoons	red gel food colour	4	teaspoons	red gel food colour
12	teaspoons	cider vinegar	16	teaspoons	cider vinegar
6	teaspoons	baking soda	8	teaspoons	baking soda

10 in	3⅓ recipes	approx. 5670 g
1500	grams	plain flour
1500	grams	caster sugar
300	grams	cocoa powder
650	grams	butter (room temp)
10		whole eggs
1200	grams	buttermilk
5	teaspoons	red gel food colour
20	teaspoons	cider vinegar
10	teaspoons	baking soda

SCALING OTHER RECIPES

I usually scale recipes up and down based on the quantities of eggs. Just note: if you have 3 eggs in a recipe you are not going to be able to halve the recipe without fart-assing around with halving an egg. Much easier to scale the recipe into multiples of 3, e.g. ⅓ or ⅔.

Another way is to add up the overall weight of the ingredients in a recipe. This will quickly tell you what size tin you need to use. These weights are for a three-layer round cake as per the Magnolia Kitchen MO. If you want square cakes, divide the weight by 3 and add that to the weight in the table (that's what we do at MK). For example, a 4 in square cake would need 800 g + 267 g = 1067 g (or 2 lb 5½ oz).

ROUND CAKE TIN SIZE (in)	AVERAGE INGREDIENT WEIGHT (FOR 3 LAYERS)	
4 in	1 lb 12 oz	800 g
5 in	2 lb 12 oz	1250 g
6 in	4 lb	1800 g
7 in	5 lb 8 oz	2500 g
8 in	7 lb 8 oz	3400 g
9 in	9 lb 6 oz	4250 g
10 in	12 lb 2 oz	5500 g

CALCULATING AND SCALING ICING RECIPES

You're welcome in advance . . . the following cheat sheets for calculating icings have been asked for *so* much after the release of my previous book. Now that I am homing in on the design of cakes for events, it seemed like a good time to put you all out of your misery and share my cheat-sheet estimates.

Like I said, you're welcome!

Remember, though—these calculations are estimates for Magnolia Kitchen, used with my recipes in my Sweet Cafe to create cakes that are Magnolia Kitchen MO. This means that all quantities are based on cakes that are three layers, with two layers of filling, measuring approximately 5–6 inches (13–15 cm) tall in total with icing. If you are not using my recipes or you are making cakes that are not Magnolia Kitchen MO, then sorry, loves, I can't help you hehe!

ALSO: THESE ARE ESTIMATES ONLY! Please remember this when you happen to have icing left over, or maybe you don't have quite enough icing and you need to whip up a little more. Estimates can only do so much, right?

The ganache ratios are specifically designed for icing cakes. I recommend using compound chocolate as I have always found it sets more solid than standard chocolate, giving a better structure at room temperature. If you choose to make your ganache for icing your cake using couverture chocolate, all the luck to you in your off-script adventure. Also, the cream needs to be at least 35% fat content.

Cake sizes are in inches and ingredient weights in grams . . . see page 238 for why. The quantities are for one three-layer cake at each size.

GANACHE FOR ICING

ROUND CAKES (THREE LAYERS)					
CAKE SIZE (in)	**GANACHE 1:3**		**GANACHE 1:4**		**TOTAL WEIGHT (g)**
	Cream (g)	Dark compound chocolate (g)	Cream (g)	Dark compound chocolate (g)	
4	168	503	134	536	670
5	227	681	182	726	908
6	293	880	235	938	1173
7	366	1099	293	1173	1466
8	447	1340	358	1430	1788
9	534	1602	427	1709	2136
10	628	1885	503	2010	2513
CAKE SIZE (in)	**GANACHE 1:4**		**GANACHE 1:5**		**TOTAL WEIGHT (g)**
	Cream (g)	White compound chocolate (g)	Cream (g)	White compound chocolate (g)	
4	134	536	112	558	670
5	182	726	151	756	907
6	235	938	195	977	1172
7	293	1173	244	1222	1466
8	358	1430	298	1489	1787
9	427	1709	356	1780	2136
10	503	2010	419	2094	2513

SQUARE CAKES (THREE LAYERS)					
CAKE SIZE (in)	**GANACHE 1:3**		**GANACHE 1:4**		**TOTAL WEIGHT (g)***
	Cream (g)	Dark compound chocolate (g)	Cream (g)	Dark compound chocolate (g)	
4	200	600	162	648	810
5	275	820	219	878	1097
6	355	1060	284	1134	1418
7	443	1329	354	1418	1772
8	540	1620	432	1728	2160
9	645	1936	516	2066	2582
10	759	2278	608	2430	3038
CAKE SIZE (in)	**GANACHE 1:4**		**GANACHE 1:5**		**TOTAL WEIGHT (g)**
	Cream (g)	White compound chocolate (g)	Cream (g)	White compound chocolate (g)	
4	162	648	135	675	810
5	219	878	183	914	1097
6	284	1134	236	1181	1417
7	354	1418	295	1477	1772
8	432	1728	360	1800	2160
9	516	2066	430	2152	2582
10	608	2430	506	2531	3037

* The 1:3 ratio doesn't *quite* add up to these numbers, but it won't matter. Trust me.
See also overleaf for more detail on ganache ratios.

BUTTERCREAM FOR ICING

The buttercream cheat sheet below can be used for all of my buttercream recipes—Swiss, Italian, German and my newbie French . . . *bienvenue*. PLEASE don't use this for American buttercream —you know how I feel about it, and if you use the cheat sheet for that *yuk* nasty icing I will feel it deep in my heart no matter where you are in the world.

All of my buttercream recipes tell you how much one full recipe makes, so you can work out how to divide or multiply to get the approximate amount of icing you need. Again, this cheat sheet is for Magnolia Kitchen MO three-layer cakes.

CAKE SIZE (in)	ROUND CAKES BUTTERCREAM (g)	SQUARE CAKES BUTTERCREAM (g)
4	500	900
5	850	1200
6	1200	1500
7	1570	1950
8	1950	2450
9	2350	2900
10	2750	3400

GANACHE RATIOS

———

While we're on the subject of icing, I'm going to give you the lowdown on ganache ratios AGAIN, because you might need it if you're scaling some of my recipes. This info appeared in my first book, but I guess there's a *small* chance that some of you haven't got yourself a copy yet . . .

Ganache can be made in different ratios of chocolate to cream, and is allowed to set for different times depending on what you're using it for. A ratio of 1:2 means 1 part cream to 2 parts chocolate.

DARK CHOCOLATE GANACHE RATIOS
- 1:1 for a glaze
- 1:2 for cake filling and piping
- 1:3 for covering cake (if stored at room temp)
- 1:4 for covering cake (if stored at room temp in the heat of summer)

WHITE CHOCOLATE GANACHE RATIOS
- 1:1 for a glaze
- 1:2 for cake filling and piping
- 1:4 for covering cake (if stored at room temp)
- 1:5 for covering cake (if stored at room temp in the heat of summer)

SETTING TIMES FOR VARIOUS USES
- For a glaze, use straight away.
- For filling and piping, allow to set at room temp until the ganache is spreadable, like room-temp butter.
- For covering cakes, I like to prep my ganache and allow it to set overnight, then reheat it to a spreadable consistency as needed. Once you've made your ganache, grab a baking tray that is at least 5 cm (2 in) deep and line it with plastic wrap. Pour your ganache into the tray, then cover tightly with plastic wrap. Ensure the wrap is pressed flat against the ganache so that no air can get in and make it crusty. This method makes reheating a bloody dream: simply remove the plastic wrap, transfer the ganache to a chopping board and use a sharp knife to cut the ganache into cubes of about 2.5 cm (1 in). Place in a suitable bowl and heat in the microwave in bursts: 1 min then stir, 40 secs then stir, 20 secs then stir, then repeat in 20-sec bursts until the ganache is a spreadable consistency.

MAKING THE RIGHT AMOUNT
Obviously, different ratios make different amounts of ganache. You can use the handy-dandy tables on page 252 to help you make the correct amount of ganache for your cake.

ACKNOWLEDGEMENTS

Wow, who knew I would be doing this again?

TO MY FAMILY: Harley, who is always my team no matter what, supporting me through the ups and downs and just keeping our family moving forward. I am the luckiest woman in the world to have the family I have. I just want to say: Harley, Charlotte, James and Edward, you are my world and I promise to show you that always!

TO ALLEN & UNWIN: Shit, you guys picked up a random (me, circa 2017) and gave her a publishing deal. Both parties had high hopes but didn't really know what to expect, and now I am on book number two!! I can't thank the team at A&U enough for your faith in me and in our shared success. Jenny, Leanne and the whole gang, you really are amazing. I know I stress y'all out, but I get there in the end hehe. Also let's not forget the freelance editorial team of Teresa, Kate and Sarah, as well as designer Megan, who took everything I threw at her (check out those tables).

TO PHOTOGRAPHER LOTTIE HEDLEY: Lottie, watching you with a camera and lights is so cool. I see what your face and hands do when the light or a subject needs to be adjusted, and now I know for myself what you mean. I am so happy to have had the opportunity to work on a second book with you.

TO MY STAFF: Well, the staff list has got hella long since the last book: Charlotte, Sam, Abby, Serena, Suyen, Zac, Vivian, Zoe, Danica and Abi!! My cake-fluffing team has grown and changed, and so has Magnolia Kitchen, but the size of the team will never change the fact that we are a family. Each and every one of my staff, past and present, has been pivotal to the Magnolia Kitchen journey. I have learned so much along the way— especially about myself as a boss! Thanks, guys, you literally rock my world. Your support, hard work and faith in my visions is never-ending!

TO MY COMMUNITY: Y'all get me every time! Every customer who walks through the door or makes a purchase online; every person who writes an email or posts a comment or sends a DM on social media. Those personal connections and online interactions are all so, so important to me, and so important to Magnolia Kitchen. I say it a lot and it is never any less true, so I will say it again: Magnolia Kitchen and I wouldn't be diddly-squat without your support!!

I'm sure I've left out some people, so if that is you please don't be offended that I am including you in the blanket THANK YOU. Bets xx